© 2022 Sarah Phillimore and Al Peters

P&P Publishing

Transpositions

Personal journeys into gender criticism

Compiled and edited by Sarah Phillimore and Al Peters.

All rights reserved. No part of this publication may be reproduced, distributed, or transmitted in any form or by any means, including photocopying, recording, or other electronic or mechanical methods, without the prior written permission of the publisher, except in the case of brief quotations embodied in critical reviews and certain other noncommercial uses permitted by copyright law.

Cover illustration, design and book layout by Al Peters@2cheeseburgers

* * *

With thanks to Caz Bailey and Doug Fisher.

Transpositions

Personal journeys into gender criticism

Transpositions

Contents

Story	Author	Page
Foreword	*Graham Linehan*	11
Introduction	*Sarah Phillimore*	13

Transpositions - part I

1	Peak trans	*Anon*	19
2	TERFed out of a career	*Kara Dansky*	24
3	I am not going to be quiet	*Ali*	29
4	A TERF is born	*Gina Scott*	32
5	The rose-tinted glasses fell off	*Anon*	33
6	Initially, I was supportive	*MJ*	36
7	Watching The TERFS	*Anon*	37
8	We are braver	*Alison*	41
9	The spark	*Anon*	42
10	Branching out	*Mel*	44
11	Thanks a Bunce	*Anon*	45
12	A sledgehammer	*Jenny*	46
13	Angry, from Edinburgh	*Carol Bailey*	48
14	My autistic daughter declared a trans identity	*Anon*	51
15	I am a male Trump supporter	*MAGA ally*	53
16	Gaslit, coerced and oppressed	*Anon*	55

Contents

	Story	Author	Page
17	The peakening	*A Heartbroken Mother*	56
18	Shut up and get on with it	*Anon*	58
19	The adult babies takeover	*BigBillMoon*	59
20	Dyfal donc a dyr y garreg	*Fran*	62
21	It had to be fought against	*Anon*	64
22	I thought the war was won	*Sarah*	66
23	A cry, a promise and a truth	*KDP*	67
24	It's better to be rude…	*@mairijcam*	68
25	We are angry… and informed	*Anon*	70
26	Self ID is a regressive step	*Anon*	73
27	I don't call myself non binary anymore	*Anon*	75
28	I felt outrage	*Anon*	76
29	I was buying 'be kind'	*Anon*	77
30	Germaine to our argument	*Anon*	78
31	TERF journey	*G. Wilson-Stonestreet*	79
32	Grumpy, radical feminist	*Andreia Nobre*	81

Gallery - Pictures from TERF Island 83

Transpositions - part II

33	The eve of the war	*Al Peters*	96
34	Homesick blues	*Carol*	103
35	The situation spiralled rapidly	*Anon*	105
36	Overwhelmed with information	*Anon*	107

Contents

	Story	Author	Page
37	Incandescent	*Frankie*	109
38	In the name of trans	*Shazz*	111
39	I cannot be silent	*Tracey*	112
40	Doing my bit	*Louise*	114
41	Take that purity spiral and…	*Delyth*	115
42	A lifetime of male abuse	*Anon*	117
43	The seven peaks	*Anon*	121
44	Finding out	*Catherine*	127
45	Like an avalanche	*EO*	129
46	So many rabbit holes	*Helen*	130
47	The price we pay	*Sarah P.*	131
48	The beginning of hell	*A*	132
49	Secretive	*Elizabeth*	133
50	Women won't wheesht	*@Dis_critic/Wheeshtcraft*	134
51	I am not going to be quiet	*Anon wife*	136
52	Good knight	*Anon husband*	138
53	An active voice	*Melanie*	139
54	The awakening	*Wendy*	141
55	One thing every day	*Pauline*	143
56	Dinosaurs, and nothing pink	*Anon*	146
57	Back into the ring	*Anon*	148
58	Fighting for my lost freedom	*Anon*	149
59	Every single thing makes a difference	*Tracy Duckett*	151
60	Where does this come from?	*Anon*	153
61	A bunch of aggressive lunatics	*Cycledance*	155
62	Staff diversity	*Anon*	156
63	I googled Susie Green	*Anon*	159

Contents

Story	Author	Page
Tweet section	*Various contributors*	163

Transpositions - part III

64	She	*Her mother*	177
65	Genderfeels are a luxury	*Anandamide*	180
66	Slow burn	*Concerned Mother of 3*	181
67	For Fox sake	*Siri J. Bodin*	183
68	A bubble of woke	*Anon*	184
69	When the dysphoria fades	*CJ*	186
70	No thank you	*Wendy*	191
71	Brighton sock	*Anon*	194
72	Peaked, working for the NSPCC	*Anon*	196
73	The long good 'why'	*S*	199
74	Another side of things	*MJ Austen*	202
75	It's a big hill to die on	*Anon*	203
76	Birth of a TERF!	*Anon*	204
77	A can of worms	*MsChopsy*	206
78	Friends, lost and found	*Anon*	208
79	The shifting Sands	*Kelly W*	209
80	The mess we're in	*Jen*	210
81	Here's the thing: I am scared	*Anon*	211
82	Nope!	*Sandra Taylor*	215
83	Common sense will prevail	*Anon*	216
84	Wax on, wax off	*Anon*	217
85	What this TERF has to say	*Anon*	218
86	Enter Mumsnet!	*Anon*	221

Contents

	Story	Author	Page
87	I didn't want to be a coward	*Anon*	222
88	A dent in my certainties	*Anon*	224
89	I saw womanhood as a club	*Anon*	226
90	Exhausted, stressed and fearful	*Anon*	228
91	The cotton ceiling	*Aja*	230
92	A chilling response	*Anon*	231
93	Steppin' out over the line	*Ally*	232
94	This is not how we should treat children	*Anon*	234
95	Reality denied	*Anon*	239
96	Alienated	*Anon*	242
97	Radicalised for the first time	*Anon*	244
98	Throwing his weight around	*Rex Landy*	246
99	Can you live with yourself?	*Anon*	247

* * * *

100	A safer world	*JH*	254
101	Getting away with it	*Liz*	257
102	Asking questions	*Phil*	258
103	A new Victorian attitude	*Women's Action Group, Australia*	260
104	Watching and learning	*Anon*	261
105	Had enough	*Anon*	263
106	The day I found my rage	*MrMenno*	265
107	Stalin's 'whisperers'	*Anon*	267
108	Then the eyes of the blind shall be opened	*Hackney Terven*	270

Contents

	Story	Author	Page
109	I read everything I could find	*Anon*	271
110	O no Canada!	*Anon*	273
111	I thought Mermaids was a swimming club!	*Anon*	275
112	It is by women and by land, that the people are given life	Michelle Uriarau, Ngāti Hinepare, Ngāti Mahu, Ngāti Kahungunu	278
113	What the Dickens is going on?	*TerfyMcTerfyFace*	282
114	Fighting monsters in the dark	*Ceri Black*	285
115	Watching the TERFS	*Verdi Wilson*	292

Transpositions

Personal journeys into gender criticism

Transpositions
Personal journeys into gender criticism

Foreword

by Graham Linehan

It's a bit difficult for me to pinpoint the exact moment I peaked because, for me, peaking is a permanent state. I peak several times a day, as story after story comes in to my website from whistleblowers highlighting the absurdity, incoherence, misogyny, homophobia and toxicity of the trans movement, which is really a men's rights movement in drag. When I speak to the gay elders fighting it, like Fred Sargeant, Kate Harris and Bev Jackson, I often ask them: have you ever seen anything like this before? And the answer is always, "No. Never". It's unprecedented. A fascinating disaster, a slow-motion scandal, an unfolding tragedy. It is all these things, and I don't think I will ever become immune to the insanity.

Sometimes I tell people I peaked when my home country voted to change the Eighth Amendment and its accompanying draconian restrictions on abortion rights, and Amnesty Ireland called it 'a great victory for pregnant people'. They removed the women who had fought the war from the scene of their greatest victory. Then, the same dishonest, women-hating, fashion-chasing members of the laptop class brought in self-ID, secretly, attached to the more popular cause of marriage equality, and the big con was complete. Women were suddenly 'people'. Thus, they disappeared, and along with them, their sex-based rights.

Many within these pages cite my meagre efforts to bring this scandal to wider attention as the reason they peaked. I could not be more proud of that fact, but it's not enough. We all have to do our bit. Throughout society, there has been an ideological coup, putting the rights of women, children and gay people in terrible danger. 'To peak' is simultaneously something that happens to you, and something you do to others. Write letters to your MP, your local paper, but most importantly of all, tell your friends. Do whatever you can, as safely as you can, to get the word out.

They can't win, not long-term, but we have a fight on our hands.

Keep peaking, people, and keep peaking people.

GL

October 2022

* * * *

Transpositions
Personal journeys into gender criticism

Introduction

by Sarah Phillimore

In recent years, much of the developed world has become apparently unable to answer the question 'what is a woman?' The recognition of 'sex' as a protected characteristic has been continually undermined by an ideological movement that seeks to replace 'sex' with 'gender identity expression', on the basis that this is 'kinder' and 'more inclusive' to those who are unhappy with the sex of their birth.

Hopefully, few would deny that we should all be able to live our lives as we choose so long as we don't hurt others. No one should feel forced into ways of behaving or dressing that are based on stereotypes about what their sex could or should make them do.

But equally, few can sensibly deny that the consequences of having a male or female body are significant, fixed at conception and immutable. And for women and girls especially, there are harmful consequences from denying the existence of their sex or making it subservient to a man's claimed 'gender identity' - from refusing women access to single sex spaces and activities, where their safety and dignity is at stake or encouraging teenage lesbians into double mastectomies and a life long reliance on cross sex hormones.

It seems that the ground work for this new ideology of sex denial was laid many decades ago, but in the UK it seemed to take hold of state institutions around 2015 – around the time that the lobby group Stonewall announced it would add the 'T' to the 'LGB' and focus its fundraising around that.

Any expression of unease about what this might mean for women and girls in particular, was not merely discouraged but actively suppressed, with the police as willing accomplices. For a while it looked as if the mantras of 'no debate' and 'be kind' would sweep all before it – including child safeguarding and fundamental rights of free expression. But then people began fighting back. Some had been warning for years of what was coming, some were much more recent arrivals. The detailed history of that movement is not our focus here – hopefully there will be many learned and detailed accounts to come.

The power and reach of the printed word has been recognised for centuries – from Gutenberg's printing press in the 1400s, to the attempted murder of Salman Rushdie in 2022 because of the words he wrote in 1988. We are very grateful to those who wanted to share their stories and we hope that in this book you will find much to interest, inspire, enrage and sadden you.

Our aim was to gather the responses of women and men in their own words, to find out what it was that woke them up, or made them more determined to object, and create a physical artefact to celebrate our 'origin stories'. So much – good and bad – has been achieved on line, but so much of that is ephemeral.

Sometimes, what you need is to feel a book in your hands and hold the weight of the words.

SP

October 2022

* * * *

He who controls the language,

controls the debate.

(attr. various)

Transpositions

part I

1

Peak trans

Like many of the women involved in the fight against gender identity ideology, my starting position is that of a left-wing feminist and supporter of LGBT rights. Having become interested in politics and activism at university, I've been involved in campaigning to a greater or lesser extent most of my adult life. I like to think I've always kept myself reasonably well-informed on social and political issues.

As a woman, the primary focus of my concerns and activism has always been feminism but I've also campaigned for gay rights and equality. There was also a time I would certainly have considered and called myself a trans ally, too. I believe wholeheartedly that trans people deserve to live their lives with dignity and respect, free from discrimination and violence and with all their human rights protected by law.

But so do women.

Back when I was first finding my feminist feet in the late 80s and early 90s, I didn't see a problem with making a little space for transwomen. Perhaps it was the naivety of youth or that I hadn't quite yet shaken off the vestiges of my female socialisation but I was happy to accommodate transwomen in womanhood. Of course, I did not believe that human beings can magically change sex and I did not consider transwomen to be female but, at the same time, I did perceive them as different from men. It seemed to me that, like women, transwomen were vulnerable to harm in a male-dominated world and that we were all united in a common goal against a common enemy.

At that time, however, I think we all understood what 'trans' meant. A transsexual was someone with a formal medical diagnosis of dysphoria who struggled psychologically with their sexed bodies. They took hormones and had significant surgical alteration in order to live socially as the opposite sex.

I was happy to use female pronouns, to call trans-identified males 'transwomen' and to welcome transsexuals into female spaces such as toilets and changing rooms. They were so few in number that accommodating them in order to (yes, I admit it!) 'be kind', did not seem like a big deal. I never considered that these small concessions would eventually end with the total colonisation and subjugation of my sex. Sharing the safe harbour of the ladies' room seemed harmless enough.

Perhaps I was extremely naïve or just lucky but the transwomen I knew never made any claim on womanhood and certainly had no desire to rob women of anything. Both sides recognised their reality and biology. There was an understanding. Transwomen were grateful for the courtesy afforded to them and respectful of being in women's spaces, conscious that they were there as guests.

Now I will no longer use the term 'transwomen' but speak only of trans-identified males. I will no longer accept males into the spaces reserved for women. I will no longer use female pronouns for males. I do not care how earnestly those males believe themselves to be women and whether or not they've had surgery. No males in women's spaces. No males to be afforded women's language. Gender identity ideology has ruined the relationship between women and transsexuals. I think it's done a great disservice to genuine transsexuals as it's caused enmity between them and the very people who were and could have been their greatest allies; radical feminists like me.

I don't remember there being one Damascene moment when I reached 'peak trans'. It was more of a slow realisation or, perhaps, a whole series of minor 'peak trans' moments which snowballed into one. It began, I think, around 2015 when Stonewall added the 'T' to the LGB. This was, if I recall correctly, the first inkling I had that something wasn't quite right.

I was a bit puzzled as to why an organisation dedicated to defending the rights of gay, lesbian and bisexual people should extend its remit to include a group of people entirely unrelated. At the time, there was no blurring of the lines as there is now. Sexuality was not conflated with the concept of 'gender identity'. They were two entirely separate groups.

Around the time Stonewall adopted the 'T', I joined social media. It was mostly through social media that I became aware of what I think of now as 'gender creep'. In certain quarters a nonsense was being peddled that denied biological sex and suggested that wholly subjective and unquantifiable feelings dictate whether one is male or female. It seemed to be coming mostly from the US. I dismissed it as a very fringe thing, a tiny group of delusional fantasists who would soon be laughed out of town. But the voices grew louder, and I started hearing the phrase 'trans women are women' repeated as a mantra. It was alarming that people were increasingly not only believing this lunacy, but were enforcing it emphatically, even aggressively.

Examples that this ideology was being embraced, particularly in the US and Canada, were everywhere; Fallon Fox being allowed to beat up women in the MMA ring, bearded men like Daniel Muscato and Alex Drummond claiming so vociferously to be women and then celebrated for doing so, the fawning over a millionaire 65-year-old father of five because he spent thousands of dollars on plastic surgery and changed his name to Caitlyn… I can't remember the exact chronology of these events and examples because they came so thick and fast but the momentum with which this movement gathered speed was shocking. Males in women's prisons, males in women's sports, males taking women's roles and opportunities, males in women's groups and organisations… even my beloved Labour Party was gobbling up the Kool-Aid and allowing 'self -identified' women – i.e. males – to steal opportunities from women on its supposedly women-only shortlists. When I tried to contact my local Labour Party to protest about his insulting affront to women, I received a rude and curt reply practically accusing me of being a bigot and more or less saying if I didn't like it I could rescind my membership. (That's exactly what I did.)

I looked on with horror as the trans juggernaut gathered speed and devastated everything in its path. I felt like I was watching the naked emperor parade by, unable to speak up because most other people were cheering his beautiful new clothes. I wondered if I might be in the wrong. Had I, in the manner of Jacques Brel's *Les Bourgeois*, become exactly the sort of person I used to hate? I was nearing middle age. Had the leftie hippy grown up into a judgemental old reactionary?

Then a strange thing happened. I was involved in a women's reading group which met once a month to discuss a novel by a female writer. Members usually took it in turns to host and to suggest the books we read. It was very informal and often involved a glass or two of wine and more general chat about work, kids, partners, dating, volunteering and feminism, etc. as well as women's literature. There were about a dozen of us.

The woman who had originally started the group and did most of the organising emailed us to introduce to her friend, Isabelle, who was interested in joining. Lots of emails flew to and fro, welcoming Isabelle and looking forward to seeing her. When I turned up to the next monthly meeting, I was shocked to find that 'Isabelle' was not a woman at all but a strapping six-foot middle-aged man in a dress. He didn't appear to have undergone any physical changes apart from wearing a shoulder length blonde wig and some pink lipstick.

From the start of the meeting, he took charge, spoke over all the women in the room and dismissed any opinion with which he did not agree. Typical male behaviour, of course. He also talked (a lot) about being a lesbian, comments which went entirely unchallenged. Most of the women present looked extremely uncomfortable and fell quiet for the latter part of the meeting. Unusually, nobody wanted to hang around after the book discussion to drink more wine and chat. Everyone made a hasty exit.

I was very disturbed by the behaviour of the woman who'd introduced 'Isabelle' to the group. She was a friend I'd known for years and whose feminist principles and activism I had hitherto respected. But she had practically simpered over 'Isabelle' and pandered to his delusions of womanhood and lesbianism throughout the evening. A few days after the meeting, I had a quiet word with her, expressing my opinion that "Isabelle" was entitled to live however 'she' wished but this was a group specifically for women and 'she' should not be there. The introduction of a male would ruin the atmosphere and negate the entire point of us meeting.

The friend I'd known and respected for almost a decade practically spat at me that 'Isabelle' is a woman and I was being extremely cruel and very un-feminist and that gender is a spectrum and that I should go away and educate myself. I was horrified. I couldn't believe she was lapping up all the all the crazy rhetoric I'd seen touted around social media.

The following day I sent a brief email saying that I would

not be returning to the group. Several other members of the group later emailed me privately to say that they were also incredibly uncomfortable having 'Isabelle' around but they dare not speak up. Like me, they just left the group. I have not seen my former friend since then. (I understand that she is now the manager of a rape crisis centre where 'self-identified' women – i.e. males – are welcomed with open arms. What a vile betrayal of the women broken by male violence.)

But I did what she suggested, and I 'educated' myself. I tried make sense of this gender guff to see if I was missing something. The more I learned, the more of a TERF I became. It soon became obvious that this was not about trans people. I discovered that, like "Isabelle", most so-called 'transwomen' are fully intact males who never intend to have any medical treatment or physical alteration. The so-called trans community was being infiltrated to the point of saturation by autogynephiles, fetishists, conmen, porn-addled incels, and any vaguely feminine bloke trying to make out his liking for sparkly earrings makes him 'gender fluid'. They were all now covered by the 'trans umbrella' as endorsed by Stonewall. I found that trans now means *everything and nothing at all.*

Everything I read and observed pointed only one way – that this is a dangerous and anti-science ideology being driven by those with the very worst motives. It is also deeply homophobic, misogynistic and anti-woman.

I quickly learned that the loudest voices in this debate are, not surprisingly, male. Gender identity is a gift to all the males who've been seething with resentment over the gains made by feminism in recent years but have had to bite their tongue and pretend. Now they have been given *carte blanche* to express their misogyny and put women back in their place.

It's also the perfect Trojan horse for paedophiles and predators who've found a way to erase boundaries and safeguarding protocols. And it's the perfect vehicle for those men who desire validation and participation in their particular fetishes. When else has a straight man been able to 'LARP' (Live Action Role Play) as a lesbian and claim the moral high ground when his sexual advances are rejected?

Learning about the rocketing numbers of children presenting at gender clinics and being pumped full of hormones terrified me. Like so many people, it is probably the aspect of this whole situation I find the most horrifying. While I'm not one for conspiracy theories, it's hard not to see the influence of *Big Pharma* corps in the promotion of this ideology. Turning kids into lifelong medical patients reliant on synthetic hormones is one helluva of a business model. I couldn't believe how easily an ideology was driving policy and children were being medicalised and experimented upon without, seemingly, anyone questioning the narrative.

Moreover, I saw that this ideology is rooted in regressive stereotypes. We're expected to believe that there are right and wrong ways to be a man or a woman, even right and wrong ways to feel being a man or a woman. That if we don't adhere to narrow and constricting rules of masculinity or femininity, we can't be male or female and need new words with which to describe ourselves. It is the ideology that is horrendously reactionary, not those who oppose it. I knew I was right.

Then, in 2016, thanks to Maria Miller MP and the Women and Equalities Committee, wheels were put in motion to not only make gender identity a protected characteristic under the Equality Act but to allow people to legally change their sex by self-declaration alone. It seemed that very soon any man would legally be a woman just by saying so.

This lunacy is the greatest threat to women's rights and safety I have ever seen.

Joining the resistance was not really a choice, it was a necessity.

• • • •

Anon

2

TERFed out of a career

I can't remember a time when I didn't think of myself as a feminist. When I was 13, my best friend and I wrote a letter to the Speaker of the U.S. House of Representatives, asking him to scrap the Hyde Amendment (a federal law that prohibits the spending of public money on abortions); my friend and I thought it was dumb that poor women should not be allowed to get an abortion. That law is still in effect. In college, I was active in the women's centre and abortion clinic defence. We held *Take Back the Night* rallies and created a task force to end campus sexual violence (after a friend's boyfriend - without her knowledge or consent - filmed her having sex with him and showed the film to his fraternity brothers). In law school, I took breaks from the demands of studying to volunteer at the National Abortion and Reproductive Rights Action League (NARAL). These days, NARAL has been captured by the cult of gender. This is what I had to say about that.

I studied radical feminism in college and law school. I was persuaded by its arguments, but I never particularly felt a need to call myself a radical feminist. I knew I was a feminist, but I wasn't particularly concerned with what kind of feminist I was.

After law school, my career took a turn. I became a public defender, ran the criminal justice centre at Stanford Law School, and worked at the ACLU, campaigning to end mass incarceration and police militarisation. I worked at various government agencies. For a while, I ran my own consulting firm, contracting with various NGOs doing legal research, policy analysis, and writing on various topics like drug law reform and getting ICE to stop using local police forces to deport people.

Three things happened in 2014 that would end up changing the course of my life:

1. *I left my abusive partner.*
   2. *I left the ACLU and planned to move to New York to start a new life.*
   3. *I learned about the threat that "gender identity" poses to women and girls.*

I provide all of this context because those three events are inseparable for me.

At some point in 2014, I realized that my 10-year relationship was emotionally and psychologically abusive. I didn't have the terminology for it at the time, but when I did even a little bit of research, I realized that it was a textbook case. The lies, the manipulation, all of it. I begged him to get help. He refused. When I started using the word 'abuse' to describe his behaviour, his anger increased. One night, it got physical. I still wasn't sure what to do. I told a friend about all of it on the phone and she said something that I will never forget. She said:

I'm going to say something that is probably going to make you very angry, and I'm willing to take that risk. I realize that you may never speak to me again, and if so, I can live with that because your life is more important to me than our friendship. You have to get out because if you don't, he is eventually going to kill you.

I started making plans to leave and in November of that year, I did.

Later in that same month, that same friend and I were talking in my apartment. We talked about everything - politics, cooking, walks in the park. I had never been much of a 'trans rights activist', but I also hadn't thought much about the topic. I just thought that 'trans' meant something like 'gender non-conforming', and I knew that I supported non-conformity with sex-based stereotypes. I said something about 'trans rights' and she stopped me in my tracks. She said, "Everything about trans is anti-woman."

I was puzzled because I had never heard that before, and I asked her to elaborate. She said, "Think about it, Kara, it's the ultimate penetration of our bodies by men." I no longer think of it in those terms (because no one changes sex), but still, the statement stunned me and all of a sudden, it all made sense.

After my friend left, I took all of my old radical feminist texts down from the bookshelf and pored over them. I took them with me when I moved to New York and consulted them frequently. I started a radical feminist meet-up group, where I met a woman who introduced me to the Women's Liberation Front (WoLF). I read everything I could find online about 'gender identity' and the threats that it poses to women and girls. I read Mary Daly and Andrea Dworkin. I joined WoLF in 2015 and became a member of the board of directors in 2016. I left the board of WoLF in 2020 (I remain a loyal member) and started working with Women's Declaration International (WDI). I'm the current president of the U.S. chapter.

Although I didn't know it at the time, by 2017 or 2018, I would effectively 'TERF myself out of my career'. I was an independent consultant at the time, working on a really interesting project involving the criminal justice rights of immigrants at the border. One day, my contractor told me that she had to pull me off of the project because the ACLU of Texas had reported that my presence on the project was 'toxic' because of things that I had said publicly about sex and gender (some might say because of my 'gender critical beliefs'). She didn't want to do it, but she said she had to. I told her that I understood, which was true. I did. So I lost my primary source of income. Later, I would go to work at a DC criminal justice agency. I resigned from that job in early 2020 because woman-haters had spent a tremendous amount of time harassing my boss for having a TERF on staff because of things that I had said about the topic during non-work hours. I had a choice: remain in my job and shut up about women's sex-based rights, or quit. I stand by my choice to leave. It was not unlike leaving my abusive partner. I had a choice: *shut up or get out.* On both occasions, I chose to get out. I'm fortunate that in both instances, my circumstances made those choices possible; lots of other women are not so lucky.

A woman recently asked me how I feel about TERFing myself out of my career. Without thinking too much about it, I responded something like, "There are many things that I am not good at, but some things I am good at are legal and policy analysis, writing, and public speaking. If the so-called 'progressive' criminal justice reform movement doesn't want to employ those skills to advance its goals, I'm happy to put them to work for women and girls."

Although I answered her question without deliberating on it too much, it was, and remains, totally true.

I started calling myself a TERF when I published my book ***The Abolition of Sex: How the "Transgender" Agenda Harms Women and Girls*** in November 2021, seven years after waking up to the harms of 'gender identity'. I have no qualms about this today, though I completely understand why many women reject the label as pejorative. I am proud to stand with the *TERF Collective, Keep Prisons Single-Sex*, and all of the other amazing grass-roots groups that have popped up in recent years, as well as WDI and WoLF - groups that remain uncompromising in their defence of women's sex-based rights. I recently published this piece about the relevance of the term TERF in today's U.S. political climate.

I no longer call myself 'gender critical'. I understand the political and legal salience of the phrase in the UK (and I am ever grateful to Maya Forstater, who I had the pleasure of meeting in person in 2019, for suing the pants off of the nitwits who refused to renew her contract because she knows that sex matters).

I'm a staunch radical feminist and I adhere to the WoLF principle that 'gender is a hierarchical caste system that organises male supremacy' and that it cannot be reformed but must be abolished. As far as I am concerned, being 'critical' of it is not sufficient. Nonetheless, as I said, I understand the political and legal salience of the phrase in the UK and I appreciate the organisers of this project for doing it. All of our stories are important and worth documenting.

Today, feminists in the USA are still behind the UK in terms of beating the 'gender identity' industry, or, as someone recently referred to it on Twitter, the 'men's rights activism corporation.' But we're not far behind you, Brits.

We're all in this together, and we're all going to win.

• • • •

Kara Dansky
U.S. radical feminist
Ohio native, Washington DC resident.

(Kara's book is: 'The Abolition of Sex: How the "Transgender" Agenda Harms Women and Girls'. Also available on Audible)

3

I am not going to be quiet

I don't have a 'peaking story'. I never believed in the first place. But I do have a story about how I came to have skin in the game, so to speak.

My brother is nine years younger than me. So I can remember everything vividly. He was always a very quiet child, thoughtful and very, very intelligent. He was bullied even in primary school, singled out because he wasn't into football and wrestling (*Raw* on Sunday morning TV was a must watch for his peers). He liked folk music (he could build a banjo from a sweet tin and a lump of 2x4), rock climbing and canoeing.

Secondary school was heart-breaking to watch. He was so alone every day, the other kids would spit in his food, steal his coats and physically assault him. The school did nothing except isolate him, rather than the bullies. This is a story that can be heard in every school in the country, sadly.

He immersed himself in an online world - and who could blame him? I have since discovered from a very good techy friend that he was in a seedy world of adult transsexuals grooming him, pointing him towards some of the most vile porn I have ever seen (he left his old computer at home when he left). He never showed any signs of femininity at all (he will lie now and say he always did - but he didn't).

At college he was studying basic engineering with the aim of going to university to do aeronautical engineering. It was at college that he 'came out' as transgender. I was in London at this time and he phoned me. I was in the pub at a friend's birthday. I'll never forget the words he said, "Al, I want to be a woman", and I just said, "ok", and hung up on him. I couldn't deal with it in the pub. A week later I was home, and we talked. He told what I now know is the usual bullshit of "I've always felt this way", "Born in the wrong body", etc.

Meanwhile my mum was broken - and I mean *broken*. But she tried to understand. Even her and my dad saying the old mantra, *better a living daughter than a dead son.* But they both knew it was nonsense. The worst was when my mum got called into the college to discuss the changes of name and 'gender' etc, on the college forms (a doctor has not even been seen yet). One of the college tutors tried to compare his coming out to her coming out as a lesbian. My mum tells me she asked how many body parts she had to chop off for that.

No one could breathe in the house in case we said something wrong, as he would just lose his mind entirely. Anyway, he passed his college exams and got accepted into four universities. He chose Brighton... *quelle surprise.*

In the summer between college and university he finally went to see a doctor (with my mum), and told the doctor he had gender dysphoria and needed hormones. He had absolutely no assessment whatsoever according to my mum, just a 20-minute appointment explaining the referral process for GIDS (The NHS Gender Identity Development Service).

This is almost 10 years ago, so the waiting lists were much lower then than they are now. So, a few weeks later he got a letter from the Tavistock Centre to say that they had received his referral and an appointment for a month later had been made. He refused to allow any of us to go with him, so off he went on a train to London (we live in Cumbria) to see the GIDS people.

He came home the next day with a hormone prescription. I don't know what lies he told to get them so quickly, but he got them. We were all absolutely horrified. But there was nothing we could do at all - as he was an adult at 19.

I started researching the affects these hormones would have on his body, not because I necessarily thought he was wrong, but I, like everyone else, thought he should have years of therapy to rule out any other mental health issues. Due to his teen years there was no doubt whatsoever he suffered with depression and anxiety but this was never looked into. He went to university and just over a year later I had my first son. That Christmas was the last I've ever seen or heard from him.

He came home for this particular Christmas and everyone tried, and I mean everyone. But it was so utterly awkward. Apart from putting on a very ill-fitting dress, he was just him - my brother, but in a dress. When it was time for him to return to university, my dad came home from dropping him at the coach station and he broke down. He said he thought that was the last time we would ever see him.

He was right.

For years I thought it was me that was completely nuts. Everywhere I went to ask the questions of how this had happened so fast, I was met with accusations of transphobia and bigotry. I was called a liar, because apparently there was no way on earth he was given hormones that fast (that still happens today when I tell people). It is only in the last few years I've found other people online with the same or similar experiences and I've realised I'm not actually nuts. I was, and am, right.

My brother suffered with extremely bad mental health due to bullying, a very warped sense of what a man must be (all the men in our family are rugby playing, pint drinking, fishing, shooting MEN!) But then so am I... *LOL.*

It was throughout all of this, I realised the danger to women's rights. The danger to young children. The insidious nature of gender ideology.

My brother was stolen, my mother is heart-broken, my dad is silent. I am not going to be quiet.

· · · ·

Ali

4

A TERF is born

I had been on Mumsnet for about 13 years. During that time I supported campaigns like 'Let Toys be Toys' and 'Let Clothes be Clothes' against genderising toys and clothes and encouraging free expression for kids. I felt that I couldn't go from supporting the campaign to let boys and girls play with any toy and resist sexist stereotyping to thinking liking girly toys makes a boy a girl.

It goes against all the fighting against sexism I've known and done all my life.

I began to notice the odd stooshie (a row or an argument) on the boards about transphobia and I realised something was up. But mostly I ignored it. Some of the posters I really respected were being called transphobic. During this time I went on Twitter to follow Tour de France people and 'fangirl' Mark Cavendish. I followed beloved comedy writer Glinner as an aside and his timeline totally peaked me. I started threads on Mumsnet about it, and then went to the *Bin the Bill* protest at Holyrood in March 2020.

...and a TERF was born.

. . . .

Gina Scott

5

The rose-tinted glasses fell off

I grew up around the art scene, went to a university of the arts and was quite submerged in what was back then seen as 'being a social outcast'. 2013 was a pretty laid back time for this sort of community. I was used to mingling with people from all walks of life and various lifestyles, I even worked circuits on the vaudeville scene - so my mentality was always a case of 'just let people be who they are' back then. I was at the time incredibly sympathetic to the trans community - after all, no one should feel unsafe or be attacked for how they are perceived in the world.

I didn't really keep tabs on what was going on over the years. I was as incredibly naive as I was in my early 20's. I eventually left the vaudeville scene and began my career in mental health. The moment my eyes were really opened to what was REALLY going on was back when J. K. Rowling's first apparent 'transphobic' tweet was all that anyone could talk about. I've never been one to take someone else's word as 'gospel' and so I went looking for the incriminating tweet - except I didn't find anything transphobic.

What I did find was a woman expressing her concerns about the implications on safeguarding and women rights with the current direction the trans community were heading. Needless to say, I was really confused by the vitriol she was receiving; she never incited hate against the trans community, she simply highlighted the importance of single sex spaces. I fully agreed with what she put; safeguarding is such an important part of my job after all. I began questioning myself. I didn't feel acknowledging sex was transphobic, yet here were many people angered by the mention of it. The sheer number of tweets with threats on her well-being and in damning her were terrifying.

In my search for answers, I began doing a bit of a deep dive. I discovered that most transwomen do not have 'bottom surgery', which was something I always believed to be the case.

Then I found out intact transwomen were getting transferred to female prisons and was mortified. As someone who has worked with both perpetrators and victims, it's very well known that perpetrators will say and do whatever they can to access potential victims and, statistically speaking, a high proportion of female prisoners are victims of violence and are at risk of further victimisation due to their vulnerability.

Around this same time I stumbled across the sports debate. I was floored by the science-denial and the dismissal of differences between the sexes. As someone who had to study anatomy and physiology extensively, it's very well documented there are biological differences between the sexes which would provide a male body advantages over females. I then noticed just how far this agenda stretched; women being silenced for speaking out about their concerns, fears and for telling their stories. Detransitioners were being harassed for telling their stories too. Anyone who wasn't fully on board with the narrative was having their lives and livelihoods threatened. Lesbians were being attacked for being same-sex attracted, the change in definition of homosexuality, black women being used as arguments for why men should have access to single sex spaces - the ball just kept rolling.

I began seeing a rise in patients who identified as Trans - something that was incredibly rare during my career before this time, most of whom had extensive histories of trauma or were neurodiverse. Interestingly it was predominantly very young women.

I began experiencing more open misogyny than I ever had in my life; being spoken over by men and women alike if I stepped out of line. Fortunately this was not the case at work as we had all noticed the drastic change in patients and hypothesised that their history may have been a factor.

I began noticing that outdated stereotypes were again being pushed; that what makes a woman is 'boobs, makeup and skirts', that being a woman was purely a feeling. This left me feeling incredibly invalidated and caused somewhat of an identity lapse for me; if a woman is just a feeling, how was I able to talk about my lived experiences or that of female patients in a meaningful way? How could I advocate for my female patients and their needs if sex no longer mattered? If everything we had experienced because we are women, no longer could be classed as such, what could we do? How could I address their needs and help them with their issues?

I became incredibly bitter about the whole situation. I felt like I was failing my patients as I saw them embrace gender rather than explore and heal from what they were going through. I felt bitter about having others tell me what it is to be a woman when they were born as men and would never understand or appreciate the things I have had to face simply on the basis of being born a woman. These experiences didn't happen to me due to my *expression* - but because of my *sex*. I felt bitter about watching women lose opportunities and resources that were put aside for them in favour of men who identified as women. I felt bitter that the idea of woman was quickly becoming something I did not resonate with due to not conforming with the stereotypes presented; I'm not submissive, 'sexy' or here to cater to the needs of men. Instead, I'm a person of authority, who rarely wears make-up and who many would call outspoken.

I felt as if the rose tinted glasses well and truly fell off and I was faced with the fact that the trans community I knew when I was a young art student had grown into a movement that was entitled, toxic and lacking in boundaries. I often wonder if it was always really that way or if it was taken over by those with malevolent intent? Gender ideology now symbolises supremacy, oppression, misogyny and homophobia to me.

My only hope is that people realise the harm it has caused and will continue to cause before it's too late.

· · · ·

Anon

6

Initially I was supportive

About 3 years ago, a close friend of mine and my husband's decided to adopt a trans identity in his 30s. Initially, I was supportive, because he was a good friend of over 15 years, and I also was still under the assumption that 'transgender' was just a mental illness.

Once our friend started taking oestrogen, his entire demeanour changed. He became obsessed with his image, and began sending us many selfies for us to fawn over. He told me that he was 'on his period', and when I reminded him that he doesn't have a uterus he curtly replied, "I don't need one to have a period".

After about a year, I was starting to get annoyed with this friend. I didn't respond to his selfies, and didn't praise him for his *womanface* attempts. One day, in a friend chat, we were talking about running and what pants to wear. I suggested he ask another male runner friend for suggestions so that he could get the right clothes that would not chafe. The trans-identifying friend said he wanted spandex leggings, and I said that spandex doesn't breathe so that might be uncomfortable.

He told me that I was 'mansplaining' to him. I realized then and there that my friend only wanted attention, and he wanted an 'oppression Olympics' to try and make himself look better.

I ended my friendship with him, and had reached 'peak trans'. After his own actions proved that he was not interested in managing his 'gender dysphoria', but rather trying to insert himself into every aspect of women's oppression, I could not take any claim of a trans-identifying person seriously. My eyes were opened to the fact that this movement is a men's rights movement.

'Listen to trans people' is the claim that activists make. Listening to trans people is exactly what turned me into a GC feminist.

Much love and support,

• • • •

MJ

7

Watching The TERFS

Let's rewind three years. I'm new to this place called Twitter. I'm finding my feet and who to follow. I like a bit of politics, so I follow a few commentators including Owen Jones. I also try and find the feminist community, a few comedians and off I go.

I soon notice that the feminists are really angry about something. They have a *bee in their bonnet* about trans issues. Hold on, I think. The rad-fem community have always been the kindest, most passionate of all the groups I've socialised with. They were always allies with the transsexuals and vice versa – why have they suddenly turned against them? I was disappointed, but curious, so I decided to sit back and watch from afar.

And it unfolds gradually before my eyes:

Owen Jones calls them bigots for not accepting that lesbians should suck 'female dick'. They ask Owen if he would give cunnilingus to a trans man. He calls them homophobic. He calls the women who marched, so that he could be openly gay, 'homophobic'.

I learn that every man who cross-dresses must be treated like a woman and given access to female safe spaces. Hold on, I think; everyone knows that there are a myriad of reasons men like to dress in 'women's' clothing. This has always been known. A few suffer from dysphoria, some make a living as drag queens, many are fetishists, and some have a pathological hatred of women. Why is the narrative treating them all like innocent angels?

I see many people sticking their oar in, shouting at the women to SHUT UP.

I see the *anime* avatars so beloved of the paedophiles saying that children as young as three can know their 'gender' and can choose to change sex. Because if a child can consent to a sex change then they can consent to sex. *Amirite nonces?* No surprise that these vermin want a slice of the PIE.

I see the lefty dudes shouting *'TERF'* at any woman who won't say that biology isn't real. That a dress turns a man into a woman. Go and tell your mothers that biology isn't real you utter pricks.

Go on.

Look her in the eye and tell her that everything she risked bringing you into the world meant fuck all. But will you shag a trans woman they are asked? God no, they all say. Every single one of them.

I see a young man in a pinafore claiming to be a lesbian but saying that homosexuality is transphobic. In fact, he says everything is transphobic. He is a woman's representative, with a penis, who hates women. Well done, Labour Party. I click on #girlslikeus and see account after account of grown men living out their sexual fetishes. Dressed up as grotesque parodies of what they think a woman should be, with pictures of their dicks peeping out of cheap, nylon crotchless knickers.

I see white middle-class narcissists fed up with being left out of the oppression Olympics calling themselves 'non-binary'. They say they do not identity as either a man or a woman. Well, tough shit you attention seeking twats – you can't identify out of reality. What you are wearing is non-stereotypical clothes. *Big. Fucking. Deal.* FYI – these will not protect you from getting pregnant or getting someone pregnant. I grew up in the 70s and 80s. Bowie and Boy George did it first and SO much better. Grow up and fuck off.

I see people in power too scared to speak the truth. Christ knows how we got to this. But shitting over women is always easier than standing up to entitled men. Changes to the GRA (Gender Recognition Act) erase 'woman'. Womanhood becomes a club that anyone can join and we are not allowed a say? Maybe we should rename it Masonhood? No-one would dare to mess with that baby. Anyway – huge fuck off to all the cowardly MPs who are happy to sign away women's rights because they lost their backbone at the ballot box.

I see men, who would lose their shit if they saw a 6ft man follow their daughter into a changing room, lie that they see trans women as real women. And just remember when your daughter says she wants to mutilate her body because she doesn't fit feminine standards – you were warned.

I see genuine trans people getting braver, finding each other and speaking out against this cult which makes them look like a bunch of science denying idiots. They are trans. They are proud. They know their biology. They do not want to invade women's spaces. I watch them get abuse. They are brave. I am proud to call them my sisters.

I see people tying themselves in knots trying to explain how men know what it means to be a woman over actual women. Misogyny is cool again.

I see the cult physically attacking women for daring to query changes to the law. And the woke lefty dudes telling them they were asking for it.

I see good women being questioned by police for speaking the truth. Orwellian times abound.

I see wilful denial of the reality of male violence. In the midst of #MeToo men are trying to argue that other men wouldn't pretend to identify as a woman to get access to female spaces. This blind ignorance that we laugh at the right for, has passed over to the left. "Haha at your religious indoctrination, climate change denial, racist beliefs. But, yes, I believe that a female soul can inhabit a male body, even if it sometimes leaves after psychiatric care."

I see grown men invading women's sports. They call themselves women. I call them *cowardly cheats*.

I see rapists with full male genitalia being locked up with vulnerable female prisoners. I see them raping incarcerated women. Male *feelz* overriding women's safety.

I see extremists trying to say the earth is flat, damaging trans acceptance. The vulnerable people with genuine dysphoria know this. Sadly, the narrative has been hijacked by the autogynephiles and is harmful to women, dysphoric people and the LGB community. How can they be part of a group that denies that homosexuality is real? When you have men calling themselves trans-lesbians and telling lesbians that they are transphobic, how do you not see the nasty side of trans activism?

I see a lefty comedian, whose beret must be a bit too tight, saying he changes from being a man to a woman depending on how he feels. Woman is a fancy-dress costume to the die-hard misogynists.

I see *terfisaslur.com* and read pages and pages of vile threats and hatred towards biological women. The MRAs have found a way to appear woke. Well done, lefty men.

I see women getting angry. Really fucking angry. When you tell 52% of the population that the very source of their oppression doesn't exist, that a feeling in a man's head is more important than all the sex based rights that their grandmothers and mothers fought for, then don't expect them to keep quiet.
If you still want to shout *'TERF'*, then go ahead. It is a great warning code to show you are a danger to women. So if you use it, I assume you are either very, very fucking stupid or a misogynist. Or most probably both.

I see you.

Women see you.

Once I started really noticing that something wasn't right with trans activism I felt myself going slowly mad, having constant imaginary arguments and my brain couldn't cope. I decided to put my thoughts down as a way of parking them and found that I couldn't stop. So, these blogs are a window into the mind of a normal, left-leaning, middle aged mum who has been driven mad by other's insanity.

• • • •

Anon

8

We are braver

I am involved with athletics and had followed Caster Semenya and Dutee Chand's appeals against the IAAFs rulings on testosterone levels closely. During the CS case it became clear that CS was genetically male and not female. I was particularly struck by Dorian Coleman's evidence to CAS* which focused on the socio economic impact of sport on girls' lives and the opportunities that sport presented and the unfairness of anyone born male retaking those opportunities away.

Even then though, I did not become an activist. That happened around 2018 when I became aware that lesbians were being abused and vilified at Pride events for stating the simple fact that lesbians don't have penises. Having grown up in the 1970s and 1980s I was stunned to see what I considered blatant homophobia dressed in the cloak of progressiveness. The more I read about the cotton ceiling, the more I stumbled on other issues.

By chance I got involved in a private Twitter group for Scots to organise for a Holyrood protest in early 2020. From there it has grown exponentially. These women are warriors. They have been bruised, battered but go on regardless. We are fighting for our lives.

From strangers they have become my friends, my sisters. Each and every one of us support each other every day.

Courage does indeed call to courage and I know that the majority of people agree with us. The more we speak the more others will speak.

We are braver.

• • • •

Alison

* Court of Arbitration for Sport (CAS) in Lausanne, Switzerland, Feb 2019

9

The spark

The first time anything properly sparked my interest and forced me to think about things was, I think, back in 2014. I had settled down to watch a Grayson Perry documentary entitled 'Who Are You?' (which unfortunately I can't find anywhere, only the trailer for it, so I can't be 100% sure it was the one). It was about identity and his idea was to explore people's ideas of what it meant to be themselves.

In the documentary, he met a series of people and as is standard for him, he talked to them at length about the topic. In one episode from the series, he met a girl who said she was a boy and had already made some efforts to express that via short hair, clothing, etc. She must have been about 17 or 18 perhaps.

What struck me was the tension between this girl and her mother. I had the year before become a parent for the first time and so the parental perspective was strongly in my mind. After witnessing this tiny baby grow and form, begin to develop language and a deep attachment to us as parents, I really felt the sadness of this girl's mother. The flash points for them were where she kept getting her daughter's 'new chosen name' wrong (I mean, she named her and raised her so surely this was an understandable thing for her to do). Her daughter would react strongly and emotionally each time it happened and there would be heart-breaking moments where they either argued or went silent on each other (at least this is how it felt).

Whereas previously, I had never thought much about the issue, apart from to react with, *oh, that's interesting – okay then*, and to kind of go along with it all in support, I was now questioning how sustainable such a radical shift in perceived 'identity' was for the child and the parents. Something just didn't sit right with me. And while I felt the girl's agony, in how she wanted to be (but wasn't fully being) perceived by others as a 'boy', It felt a step too far for me.

The bodily reality versus the 'felt' identity of the mind appeared to be the battleground here and it seemed that this girl was pushing for her mental perception of herself to take precedence over her material body. I can't remember if there was any talk of a mastectomy but had that been an issue at the time, it would definitely have consolidated how I felt about the situation.

This was my spark, my introduction to the gender arena and I believe, anyone who is able to think through the deeper details and processes of how a change of 'identity' impacts on the person and their wider circle of family and friends, is likely to wake up to the distorted reality gender ideology is aggressively forcing us to go along with.

• • • •

Anon

10

Branching out

I have always had sympathy for transsexuals and had worked with some trans-identified males in the past, and I have never had an issue as to how they chose to live their lives.

I was mostly oblivious to what was happening on Twitter and how self-ID was coming in under the radar. Until I saw *the* JKR tweet and looked into what was happening to Maya Forstater. I couldn't believe the levels of abuse JKR was receiving for such a reasonable tweet and I started using my main account to like tweets and comment.

Shortly after, I realised that I couldn't be sure I'd be safe if any vindictive activist reported me to my place of work, so I started an anonymous account to fully commit to this fight. I have so much admiration for the women who have put their heads above the parapet and faced down various legal issues, they are making the world safer for us all with their courage.

I am now a branch co-ordinator in the Scottish Feminist Network. Our branch hosted and organised the fantastic *Alloa Women's Festival* in March.

• • • •

Mel

Thanks a Bunce

My sister was peaked a while before me and so I have her to thank. She talked to me about the 'trans issue' from time to time and my initial reaction was 'be kind'. She persevered and talked about how so many trans-identified males have no 'bottom' surgery and are therefore, still 'fully intact' males. I heard and understood what she was saying but I still didn't really 'get it' for myself.

The hook that got me was when she told me about Pips/Philip Bunce and his women's award. Oh, and she showed me his pictures! I work in HR and fairness and reasonableness are fundamental for me. This guy cross-dressing on some days when he felt like it by wearing a pencil skirt, heels and fishnets and winning a women's award is unfair and no reasonable employer should consider him for this category.

I've been part of the Women in Banking and Finance (WiBF) organisation when I worked for a major UK bank. Thankfully when I was involved the trans topic never came up but I'm sure they include men now.

I started to connect with more GC women on Twitter and started looking into it and reading material for myself. I've never looked back.

I still want people who feel dysphoric to be able to live as healthy and happy a life as possible but humans can not change sex.

• • • •

Anon

12

A sledgehammer

I was meandering through Twitter and started to read up about what was happening to Marian Millar. I arrived at it through the ridiculousness of the 'hate speech' bill that had been pushed through the Scottish Parliament. (I didn't realised then how relevant it would be to all this Transgender ideology nonsense)

I couldn't believe that she was being witch-hunted for telling the truth, and tying ribbons in a park. And that a *grown man* appeared to be frightened of ribbons. As you do, I went onto the timeline of the trans-identified male that threw Marian and the women out of the 'Doctors' pub in Edinburgh. I don't know what I was expecting, maybe some poor guy who was genuinely struggling with his identity, like a couple of young guys I knew growing up.

It was just raging vitriol towards women, with smug comments that he had chucked women out of the pub (for wearing t-shirts that said the wearers were women), and just screeds of re-tweets of porn. This was nothing to do with genuine body dysphoria, it was just purely shemale porn, and I was aghast. I foolishly went down the rabbit hole of looking at the re-tweeters' profiles and saw the links to *OnlyFans* pages. I thought my head was going to explode. I had no idea that this was so accessible to anyone, especially kids.

I wrote to my MP, I reported it on Twitter, and even then they only removed some of the profiles. It hit me like a sledgehammer that this ridiculous gender movement is mainly porn-driven fetishism and misogyny. I didn't even know what AGP* was then, but I do now.

My second sledgehammer was what's happening to vulnerable youngsters with co-morbidities being pushed into transitioning surgically by the social media contagion. So many youngsters with mental health issues being damaged even more.

I've been shouted at in the street (on a stall) by a young female adult, who saw me as the enemy. It's going to be so hard to get these kids to realise we're trying to protect them, because they've been brainwashed.

That is just heartbreaking.

. . . .

Jenny

* AGP = Autogynephile. Autogynephilia is defined as a male's propensity to be sexually aroused by the thought of himself as a female.

13

Angry, from Edinburgh

I'm angry. In fact, I'm furious.

I am furious that the NHS can lie to a woman who was raped in hospital, and tell her that, against the evidence of her own experience, she could not have been raped as only women were present on the ward.

I am furious that girls and women are being deprived of fair competition in sports, and aren't allowed to speak about it.

I am furious that female prisoners are having to share cells and showers with rapists and abusers.

I am furious that women are self-excluding from rape crisis services in case males are likely to be present.

I am furious that children are being told that, if they don't fit in, they can become someone else, and that will fix everything.

I'm furious that women are told they are TERFS and bigots for speaking the truth.

I was angry in 2018, but for a different reason. We'd apparently voted to leave the EU, but the paperwork hadn't gone through, and I was hopeful that somehow the tanker that was Brexit could still be stopped. I wasn't paying attention to women's issues that much. I've always voted Labour, and always felt I leaned to the left, I was an avid Guardian reader, and always supported gay rights.

I am an indexer of books, mostly for university presses, and I'd seen the 'alphabet soup' grow, with not very much curiosity, but always felt some sympathy with those encompassed in that milieu, though I hardly ever came across anything related to it in my personal life. I indexed a book on transgender healthcare in early 2020, and, although I always index dispassionately, I do recall feeling some sympathy for people's struggles with their gender. I have a vague memory of listening to an early episode of the *Standard Issue* podcast. Jess Phillips either said something or was reported to have said something like, she didn't believe transwomen were women - (it is a very vague memory) - and I remember being a little disappointed in Jess, who I'd always admired prior to that.

The next thing that I remember is listening to an interview James O'Brien did with Paris Lees, and feeling very sympathetic towards Lees, and talking about the interview with 'M' (my partner), but I don't recall him showing any particular interest. The rest is a jumble of conversations in the pub - and giving a friend who said, "They aren't women though," the side eye.

I think by this time perhaps M was starting to pay attention to the subject a little, but we weren't in agreement. I was very much on the 'be kind' pathway. At this time, most of my Twitter activity was Brexit-related, and through that I followed a gay guy called Max. I always enjoyed his wonderfully sweary irreverent posts, and his infrequent, similarly very sweary podcasts. Then I began to notice he was saying awful things about Graham Linehan, who I was aware of (though I hadn't actually seen *Father Ted* by then). He called him a 'transphobe' and a 'bigot' and, I don't really know why, because I wouldn't have called myself a fan then, but I didn't like it, and I didn't believe it, so I started to look into the subject a little more.

By now M was clearly taking more notice of what was going on - he's always been way ahead of me on the gender ideology debate, but never tried to persuade me one way or the other. He has reminded me while I've been in the process of writing this that he first came to it through the Jordan Peterson pronouns/compelled speech row. We have spent a lot of time talking about it over the last couple of years, we've both read a lot on it, and now I can't imagine what the hell I was thinking.

Did I really think that transwomen are women? I don't really remember. I know I didn't have a clue about AGP (Autogynephilia) - I probably assumed that all trans-identified males were gay, which is why I was sympathetic. I still have some sympathy - mainly for the youngsters who are ruining their bodies but haven't realised it yet - the kids making videos about all the problems they're having after their surgeries - the detransitioners. I don't hate anybody, but I do think some of them have got a fucking cheek (looking at you, Willoughby).

And the more I see them taking the piss, the angrier I get, until now, when I hear someone like 'Lia' Thomas being called a 'trans woman' and she/her, I get a knot in the pit of my stomach. None of this has affected me personally yet - I'm self-employed and work from home - so there have been no work issues. I have hardly been anywhere in the last couple of years, and haven't really encountered a 'gender neutral' toilet yet. I don't know anyone who is 'trans' or 'non-binary' - so why should I care? It doesn't affect me, right?

Well, what I keep thinking is, if it gets to the stage where it does affect me, maybe then, it will be too late.

• • • •

Carol Bailey

14

My autistic daughter declared a trans identity

Most of my life passed without any need to be 'gender critical'; I have no idea when this term even emerged, or rather when the need for such a term arose.

I come from a working-class family. Nearly all of my female relatives were what might be considered gender non-conforming; they behaved in ways that came naturally to them, dressed how they liked, and some fought to get into male-dominated positions. One was a fire-fighter. One was a construction worker. Several had fought as partisans in the Second World War.

What is a woman?

Anything she damn well pleases — a message I raised my daughter with as well, not knowing that what she pleases to be might include 'a man'. I was vaguely aware of the existence of transsexuals but had never met any personally.

The first time I became aware of gender ideology was when I was participating in an internet group for parents, around ten years ago. A fellow member had discovered that her teenage son had been stealing her panties when she caught him masturbating in them. She took him to therapy. The therapist told her to support her 'daughter'. He didn't even identify as female or declare a trans identity. He said that he liked the thought of having breasts surgically implanted but had no interest in hormones. He said it was a fetish. The gender therapist insisted he was trans.

This mother sent me distraught message after distraught message, not being able to discuss her fear, worry, and panic in the larger group because they shut her down for not being supportive... again, of her 'daughter'.

After a while, this mother disappeared from the group, and I later heard that her marriage had broken down and she'd moved far away. This issue had demolished her family.

Weird, I thought, and sad, and twisted, yet still it didn't touch my everyday life in an entirely different part of the world.

Now I'm in the same boat. My autistic daughter has declared a trans identity after feeling rejected by society and living her life online during the pandemic. I've raised her the way I was raised, with an invitation to wear what she likes within the budget, and to do whatever she likes, pursue whatever interests she likes. A series of internet searches about feeling bad about life and puberty led her down this rabbit hole very suddenly, and in a very trance-like manner.

I love her. I want her to be safe. I know her. I see in her the young ideologue I once was, ready to defend her ideals to the death if need be. I am terrified. I do not believe this is an organically-formed identity. I think she is confused and hurting and trans offers 'all the answers' she so desperately wants. I'm living with someone who feels like a complete stranger, and my home feels like a verbal minefield. The upside is this — in my country, no doctor will give her surgeries and hormones until after years of very regular therapy.

I didn't join the wider debate. The 'gender critical battle' is fought within my own family, and I better not say anything, or I'm a TERF and a transphobe and 'not a good person'. I bite my tongue and I pray. I pray that I'll have my daughter back some day, beautifully non-conforming and beautifully herself, in an 'authentic self' discovered through life and not online.

I pray even though I'm an atheist, because I'm discovering that I'm powerless to do much else.

. . . .

Anon

15

I am a male Trump supporter

My story is different since I come from a different political side than most gender critical feminists but I agree with the main points. I am a male Trump supporter and my journey to becoming gender critical started in university when I heard about transgender people. I had no problem with the idea of calling someone their pronouns so long as it wasn't something weird like they/them or xe/xer.

What peaked me was Jordan Peterson and forced pronoun usage. Like I said I have no problem saying someone's pronouns but there is a difference between asking someone to say your pronouns and demanding someone say your pronouns.

My journey was completed when conversations moved towards allowing transwomen into women's rest rooms and sports. Men and women are biologically different. Men naturally have more muscle mass and to put a transwomen who has such an advantage against regular women is unfair. And as for the restrooms, I don't believe transwomen will harm women in those spaces but there will be opportunistic evil men who will pretend to be trans in order to get closer to women in a space that should be safe for them.

We Trump supporters have women that are important in our lives. Wives, daughters, and mothers. The very idea that they will have to share a restroom with a gross man getting his rocks off disgusts me. And if I ever have a daughter it saddens me that she will be at such a disadvantage in competitive sports.

Our body is a gift from God and we should be comfortable in them. I fear that if I ever have a daughter she will hate being a girl because of how twisted this world is becoming. And that makes me sad.

That is my story. I hope it isn't too long. Please keep up the fight.

There are so many that are gender critical but are scared to speak up. Thank you for your effort.

Thank you and God bless,

• • • •

MAGA ally

16

Gaslit, coerced and oppressed

What made me GC? Well, I guess I have always been, I believe in the reality of what I see with my own eyes, my experiences as a woman and biological reality.

I didn't take much notice of the debate until Hubbard entered the Olympics; a fully-intact, middle-aged male competing in the weight lifting against females in their late teens, early 20s. it sent me down a rabbit hole of things I didn't know about, things the news never speaks of.

I felt gaslighted, coerced and oppressed - a feeling I am very familiar with from past domestic abuse and which I refuse to submit to ever again. No-one is going to push me down again and mess with my mind.

• • • •

Anon

17

The peakening

People often ask, "When did you peak? What was it that made you critical of trans ideology".

Honestly, I think for me it was more of something I never really believed in but felt obligated to entertain as a liberal in good standing. It was probably 2014 when my daughter, then 14 years old started obsessing about *all things LGBTQ*. I thought it was odd being that she had never really shown any indication of being a lesbian or bisexual but I knew she was exploring and that didn't bother me. I just thought it seemed a bit unlike the kid I knew, but I wasn't particularly concerned. I knew I would love her no matter what and so would her father and her brother. And at the end of the day, it really didn't affect me - she just needed the time and space to figure things out.

When she started flirting with the idea of being 'trans' it threw me for a loop. She had never been particularly gender-nonconforming and when she would repeat the gender ideology talking points there always seemed to be a vacancy behind her eyes, as thought she was just reciting a script that had been given to her by someone else. The more questions I asked the angrier she became. I tried doing some research and at the time the consensus was that gender dysphoria tended to be 'insistent, persistent and resistant', and presented itself when a child was very young. Well, my daughter had never shown any signs and while I didn't necessarily buy into the idea that children were born in the wrong body just because they embraced stereotypes of the opposite sex, it did give me relief that she did not fit the profile.

I suppose at that time the criteria seemed to be indicative of some kind of *True Trans* and I knew my kid was definitely not that, even though I really wasn't sure what trans actually was as a coherent definition. It seemed to me everyone questioned themselves at some point in adolescence and wondered if they met the social ideals expected of their sex.

I suppose when I really hit the point of no return was when my daughter would come back from school mentioning new 'trans' kids all the time and not only kept changing genders, names and pronouns but started demanding accommodations, and if they were declined would term such refusals as abuse and 'literal violence'. That was also around the time Bruce Jenner became Caitlyn and it seemed a new celebrity came out on a regular basis and all media and entertainment industries seemed to be saturated in it. I was exhausted trying to reconcile something that made absolutely no sense and couldn't believe that someone like myself, a lifelong lefty, was now a TERF bigot who was just a stone's throw away from a card-carrying Nazi.

At some point I just didn't try to check my brain at the door anymore. I gladly embraced the title of heretic and decided I would continue to push back against it, even if it meant my own child would reject me. I could tell that with all the affirmation she got from peers and adult mentors, her mental health and behaviour continued to decline... and so did her grades. I knew our family's pro-LGB stance but refusal to believe in a gendered spirit didn't make her happy but I figured we had to hold the line and keep her tethered to reality the best we could. In the end, she decided this was the life for her and ran off to live with people who would give her all the validation she wanted in all areas of life.

I miss my child but I will never give up on her or the knowledge that reality always prevails.

. . . .

A Heartbroken Mother in a Sea of Others

18

Shut up and get on with it

I had been unnerved by what I had been hearing as regards de-transitioners' stories for a while but I only 'peaked' when my daughter - who plays for a prominent team in Scottish football - heard the voice of a male who appeared to be playing for the opposition in goal. The women and the coaches had been told nothing about the likelihood of men playing in the women's team of United Glasgow, a team which has since dissolved due to lack of players (as far as we know).

    My daughter approached her coaches who as yet hadn't been informed about the males playing and who had had a mixed reaction. Her main coach was very supportive but one of the subsidiary coaches (a female) essentially said, "We don't want the club to look transphobic... you mustn't say anything". Basically, *just shut up and get on with it.*
    I was horrified, as at the time scientific studies had been published with regards to head knocks in football and I was thinking how much is this amplified when a male skull hits a female skull. My daughter plays centre back! One of my daughter's well-meaning friends said to her, "You shouldn't say anything your University place could be in jeopardy."
    This is the kind of rubbish and nonsense young girls are up against.
    The team have since been reported and our complaint led to a shake up at the Scottish Women's Football League but that gives me no satisfaction as I feel this could very easily happen again. The investigation revealed that although there are regulations that transgender players must adhere to, in Scottish Football no one had been monitoring this.

• • • •

Anon

19

The adult babies takeover

The 15th of August 2018 was the day that I became aware of the gender nonsense. I know that for a fact because the tweet that started it all for me is still available online.

You may need to know a little about my background to understand why it took a post on Twitter from a former goalkeeper to send me off into a world of confusion, disbelief, receiving death threats and everything else that comes with being 'Gender Critical'.

I'm a socialist northern bloke, somewhere to the left of the Labour Party, but not to the extremes of the mad far left that seem to be everywhere these days. I like to think I'm sensible. I'm also mad about football. As such, I follow a lot of footballers' accounts on Twitter and several political accounts too.

The now long-retired Everton goalkeeper, Neville Southall – despite being an idol for my own team's rival club – was running a very funny Twitter account, scathing at the Tory government and Theresa May, calling them 'skeletons'. I laughed along and responded to a few things but wasn't aware of anything to do with gender identity or the whole 'trans' debate.

Then one day, shortly after posting his support for trans-people, Southall announced that his account would be taken over for the day by an 'Adult Baby/Diaper Love' activist, claiming that, "People are scared to admit to being adult babies because of stigma around it".

When I had finished laughing, I replied asking if he was serious, posting about something with such obviously paedophilic overtones. Moments later he posted his now infamous tweet.

"The adult babies takeover is off. Goodbye."

My hilarity at a former professional, international sportsman reduced to posting about adult babies soon turned to questions. Many, many questions...

What on earth was he thinking? How did he get to this point? Why did no-one stop him? What even IS an adult baby? What does this have to do with football or politics? Is 'Big Nev' himself an adult baby? What the hell is going on!?

Another of the people I followed on Twitter was Graham Linehan who, along with others, picked up Southall's tweet and joined in poking fun at the shot-stopper. I started to read more of Linehan's tweets about this and other gender ideology matters, with a mix of shock and amazement.

At that point I had no idea that anyone could think that the phrase 'transwomen are women' could be taken literally. I thought it just meant *please treat transwomen as though they were women.* Then I read story after story of men trying to enter women's spaces. Tale after tale of people being doxed and losing their jobs. Post after post about a crazed ideology that seemed to be being accepted as truth.

I also learned about detransitioners and how this ideology can often lead to the medicalisation for life for children and young adults swept up by it.

Suddenly it wasn't funny anymore.

I mean a lot of aspects of the gender ideology will remain hilarious to me, but it was also frightening at times. I was now being sent death threats for arguing that we needed to protect children. I was being dragged into arguments with people who simply refused to believe scientific facts. I had to learn to walk a tightrope of what I could and couldn't post online.

Since then, I've learned so much about this ideology and its history, the women's rights movement in general, the history of the gay rights movement, politics and policy-making, biology, genetics and disorders of sexual development, and much more besides.

More than that, I've made a lot of friends online, supporting each other in fighting back against this ideology and the misogynistic science-deniers who espouse it. And we're winning. I have no doubt about that.

    I often wonder if I'd be on this side if the adult babies' take-over hadn't been cancelled.

    So thanks, Neville, you've saved me if nothing else.

. . . .

BigBillMoon

20

Dyfal donc a dyr y garreg
(Persistent tapping breaks the stone)

Would I vote Tory? Never! Nothing would make me vote Conservative. Everything I disagree with is Tory and their leaders are monsters. That's what I thought for many years, but recently my view of politics has been mixed up and thrown in the air like confetti as I try to reconcile the rights of women and the mutilation of children with the views of politicians and their parties and now I have no-one to vote for. Ironically, before, I was a political bigot, but since becoming gender critical I am now a bigot for not being one!

The Suffragettes fought hard for women's rights but I never thought that was something I would have to battle for, even knowing that wages are still unequal, that women are still treated as inferior and even knowing how being a woman has detrimentally affected me personally. I had protested things at college but once I had children didn't consider going on marches or attending demos.

When I looked into why Graham Linehan had been banned from Twitter everything changed. Friends and acquaintances were pouring out support for trans people without question and people seemed confused about what a woman is. Anything said against trans people, even the criminals, abusers and cheats meant we were transphobic and had to be cancelled, even people like J.K. Rowling were targets with daily abuse towards them flowing like streams of maggots.

A month later I found out my granddaughter was now 'a boy' and my daughter had been to the doctor and to the school, where she was to be allowed to do boy's sports and had a new name, apparently without question. My daughter uses 'he' and 'him' and won't accept me saying 'she' and 'her' and refuses to discuss trans issues and like many parents thinks she is being kind and supportive to her child. I tread carefully as I am one of the people that might change her mind, even if slowly.

    I am in awe of all the amazing women and men who have been through courts, have stood up publicly and have put in time and effort and their lives on hold to fight these issues. Shamefully I would never have heard of most of them if it weren't for this. I would always have said I was left wing politically, but now I am a single issue voter. I have now been to protests, held banners, watched countless YouTube videos, joined online gender critical groups and am determined to do all I can to protect women's spaces and equally protect children from being drawn into a cult/fad which has taken over and leads to puberty blockers, hormones and mutilative surgery on healthy bodies. I can't immediately affect my granddaughter as she lives too far away but I can drip feed my input through my daughter, online and in person where I can.

    If we all do something we will get there.

• • • •

Fran

21

It had to be fought against

I have worked in tech for over 30 years but first started programming when I was ten years old. Being a girl who liked maths and computing seemed to be confusing for many people who, for some strange reason, felt compelled to tell me so. I have worked with sensible grown-ups and not for a Silicon Valley company so it was not until 2015 that I noticed that social media companies appeared to be socially engineering the Western world.

I started a Twitter account to follow the goings on in tech and specifically tech libertarianism. A friend of mine who knew what I was investigating said I should have a look at Sam Harris's YouTube to see what I thought. Harris was definitely not for me, but the next video that auto-played was Jordan Peterson's testimony regarding bill C-16. I went back to my tech investigation and didn't think more about it until I watched a well-respected computer science academic bullied into compliance regarding a mixed-sex toilet. He wrote something twee like, "Love is love", when the toilets at his university were made 'gender neutral' and I made a comment to someone who wrote, "They just want to pee" with, "That's not all women do in toilets". The academic responded with, "Good point" but he was immediately bullied into giving an apology. The person who did the bullying seemed menacing.
I switched to an anonymous account because it seemed prudent.

I was following more and more women who were critics of social media tech companies. I must have seen someone mention the proposed changes to the Gender Recognition Act. When the North Carolina bathroom law caused controversy I, like many others, thought that meant excluding a small number of post-op transsexuals. Not long afterwards more than one of my male colleagues in a different office were 'transitioning' and putting pronouns in their email signatures, so my immediate reaction was to think about them sharing women's facilities with me. I did due diligence and read the arguments on both sides.

I noticed how many women opposed to self ID worked in SEN, were lesbian, autistic, or both. Their arguments were well considered. Many accounts arguing for self ID had *anime* profiles, appalling pornographic content, and just resorted to name-calling or even rape and death threats. A good proportion were also autistic, or claimed to be. More than a few of the posts were unhinged.

Then we had the court cases, the key one being Keira Bell's. I looked at the numbers of referrals of girls to the Tavistock and the only explanation that makes sense is social contagion. The autism link is very personal to me. I have an autistic son with learning difficulties who could be punished for misgendering (as happened to a young man in 2020). It was also only recently that I realised that I was not just mildly autistic but classically autistic. The diagnostic criteria are based on males and it is very probable that girls would be undiagnosed and that the figure of 35% of those referred to the Tavistock being autistic is much higher. It wasn't that I was gender non-conforming, but simply *non-conforming*. I am not capable of obeying conventions that don't make sense to me be they social or religious. I can easily imagine girls wanting to become boys to avoid all the social restrictions.

As a child I had frequent querying from colleagues of my mother (a doctor) as to how could I like maths and stating that they all hated maths. What I learned from this at a very early age is that perhaps some doctors aren't all that bright but certainly that I was smarter than they were, and also that they can be very, very wrong in their conclusions. Their urge to fix is very strong and medicalising mental health issues without considering family and social pressures has become a new orthodoxy. Surgically altering the body to 'fix' the minds of young people is a terrible protocol. It has to be fought against.

• • • •

Anon

22

I thought the war was won

I'm a lifelong, left wing feminist and have always strongly rejected gender roles. I thought that's where we were heading generally in the world. In fact I thought the war was won. I knew that I was uncomfortable with men in women's sports but still wanted to hold on to my progressive credentials and be 'morally righteous'. I didn't have any clue at all about the rest of the issues around women's spaces that were being raised by feminists.

But I discovered during lockdown that I was totally unaware of what had been going on in the name of feminism, and the resulting trashing of women's rights. Eventually, I spoke up online and got shot down in flames which made me aware of the raging misogyny in the trans rights movement. I learnt a bit about what was happening in schools and wanted to look out for it in my son's school (and asked him to tell me when/if he was fed pseudoscience). It happened almost immediately with a presentation to Year 6 from the notorious Jonny Hunt. I found help on Twitter and then broached the issue with the school with help from Baroness Emma Nicholson, Safe Schools Alliance, Transgender Trend and many, many more. The school accused me of being akin to a creationist and threatened me with legal action for discussing my concerns about Jonny Hunt with other parents, but I eventually got the Governors to agree to revise the policy and not to indoctrinate kids again.

Now I am part of a parents' group which helps other parents to fight this gender identity ideology in schools, and which aims to hold schools and Gov to account - we are about to launch publicly.

• • • •

Sarah

23

A cry, a promise and a truth

I am a member of Mumsnet which I've been using for many years, almost since it started.

I wasn't living in the UK when I read about the women who went swimming to reclaim the ponds at Hampstead Heath after trans-identifying men demanded to use the women-only pond, despite there being a mixed pond open to both sexes. I followed the story via Mumsnet and other media social outlets, and became more and more concerned about what was happening in the UK and beyond.

When we moved back to the UK, I joined a group of like-minded women and we are now pushing back against the harm being done to women and children, and we will protect our single sex rights - especially in Scotland.

We have had setbacks and victories in equal measure but we will keep on keeping on as **Women Won't Wheesht!**

That is a rallying cry, a promise and a truth.

. . . .

KDP

24

It's better to be rude...

January, 2019 - I finally started using Twitter, having created my account in 2013. Originally, I was looking for information on the debate around Scottish independence. I quickly followed all the usual accounts and got very invested in the pro-independence side.

Within a couple of months, I started to see disagreements between some of the big accounts, and with *Wings Over Scotland* - an invaluable resource - being called bigoted, hateful and behind the times. To start with, I was incredibly uncomfortable with what *Wings* was saying, because of course I was full-on *'trans women are women'* at that time. But his tweets chipped away at my *#BeKind* shell and I started to see over the next few months that I might have it wrong.

The event that completely blasted the *#BeKind* shell to smithereens was Julie Bindel being attacked in Edinburgh in June 2019. I was only vaguely aware of what had happened, in terms of why she'd been there and what the meeting was about, but Twitter went absolutely mental, with two very clear and very different opposing sides. One was calling out the attack as completely unacceptable. The other, berating Julie for misgendering her attacker. The big indy supporting accounts I'd previously considered rational and reasonable were saying it hadn't really been an attack as such, and her attacker was a woman and deserved to be spoken of in those terms.

Finally, it clicked. Her attacker was a man. Those accounts I'd thought so highly of were excusing him because of his special trans identity. *A get out of jail free card.*

Initially, after peaking, I would use preferred pronouns out of a desire not to offend, but it's been some time since I realised it's better to be rude than a fucking liar (thank you for that phrase, Magdalen Berns).

Needless to say, those wonderful indy accounts now have me blocked and, due to being openly critical of gender ideology, I've lost quite a few friends. However, the new ones I've made, by way of demonstrations and the Scottish Feminist Network, more than fill the gaps.

We fight on!

• • • •

@mairijcam

25

We are angry... and informed

I was asked to share the story of when I 'peaked' - when it finally hit me that something was very wrong in the world of pink and blue flags and how women were going to lose out. I can't be too specific, as I need to remain anonymous, so I'll share what I can.

I'm a feminist. Too young to have needed to protest in the streets for abortion provision or equal pay, but studying and working in a field which is male-dominated, I was always reminded about the need to defend women's hard-fought rights, equality and to keep women and girls safe. I was aware that the 2006 Equality Act protected 'gender', but I knew it was the British way of being coy about the term sex. I had some friends (male and female) that would now would be described as 'gender non-conforming', but no labels needed to be applied – we're all a little bit gender non-confirming aren't we? Robert Smith wore more lipstick and hairspray than I ever had (and still does!). I had always enjoyed Eddie Izzard's comedy and was incredibly relaxed about him outing himself as a transvestite on stage – good for him, whatever floats his boat. I had a working hypothesis that most men probably fancied getting dressed up in women's clothing at some point in their lives, whether it be drag for a stag do or full on black lace lingerie for Rocky Horror, wearing higher heels than me. Dress how you want, keep your kinks in the closet and we'll all get along just fine.

I was aware of the American 'bathroom ban' issues, because of American friends, and I knew it was about whether 'transwomen' were allowed to use women's loos. However, back in 2015 or 2016 I was still (wrongly) under the impression that 'transwomen' were transsexuals: that is to say, males that had undergone sex reassignment surgery (inverting their penis to make a neo-vagina). I am pretty certain that I believed that the new term 'transgender' was just a re-launch of transsexual and I couldn't quite understand why there was such an uproar in the US. I had been followed into the ladies loos a couple of times by men when both a child and as an adult, and in all but one case I and the other women in the loo told them in no uncertain terms to get the f*** out. The time I was alone with a 6ft 2in male student in an empty loo was just a tad terrifying (the upside of a mainly male university course was no queue for the loo - the downside no women around to help you out). I was pretty certain I had shared ladies loos with males who were presenting (they thought) as women and I naively assumed had had surgery (such innocent times). We acknowledged each other, had an unspoken agreement that we both knew what was going on but at any time the women could change the rules back, to female-only spaces, so be on your best behaviour.

Like most women, I've been groped, flashed at (starting at the age of about seven!), had to fight off pretty determined men, but thankfully have never been raped. The unwanted penis is always what worries women most, followed by the hands and accompanying strength, so I think my undeveloped thought was that a male transvestite wouldn't, couldn't, present the same threat to women? I don't think I was aware of any other transgender discussions in my world (sport, prisons, rape crisis centres) and self ID was a distant horror, still to be unveiled.

My naivete was shattered when a person I had known pretty well for several years told me they were 'transitioning'. This was a happily-married man, not an alpha male by any stretch of the imagination, but not one I would have described as effeminate or even feminine. I had not foreseen this. He knew I was liberal politically and culturally and wouldn't get any judgment from me on how he wished to define himself. We had a long chat, he told me of his mental health issues, of the suicidal ideation, that it was 'this way or no way'. I noticed he never mentioned his wife once, nor surgery, but lots of medication. I was very sympathetic, as he knew I would be, but utterly confused about how he thought he knew he needed to be a woman to be happy – how did he know what a woman felt like? I also realised I had some homework to do to work out the etiquette of not wishing to inadvertently offend by imprecise language. I expressed a hope that he didn't experience any backlash from those that were less tolerant of people who lived differently. But then the phrase that did it for me, "it's okay, I make a pretty good woman".

It was said with a smug grin and a confidence he had absolutely no reason to assume. After being initially very concerned and supportive, the arrogance of that statement stunned me. Even then my thought was, "Well, I think I get to decide that, not you," along with, "I really don't think so, mate, but we'll see".

So, off I trotted to find out what exactly was going on and the dam burst.

That dam still shows little sign of being bricked back up, but on the upside this ideology has meant women peaking around the world, and taking no more shit. We are angry, informed and networking constantly, discussing the rights we thought had already been won once and see slipping away again.

He did me a huge favour by alerting me to what was going on globally. How years of carefully directed funding by gender identity ideologues had changed the language we use (socially, politically and legally) and women's rights had already been undermined by some mad idea that human beings could change sex (*Reader, they can't*).

As for my acquaintance?

He will always be male, claims he is a lesbian, hasn't had surgery and never did make a 'good woman'.

I was right.

• • • •

Anon

26

Self ID is a regressive step

About two years ago I first become aware through friends of the injustices to women being perpetrated by men insinuating themselves into women-only spaces taking women's accolades and opportunities. I had never heard of the legal lie that is the GRC but could understand how this might have seemed expedient.

Then I became aware of the lobbying for self-identification - a hugely regressive step. Far from being a human rights issue this would bring about the shutting down of the rights of anyone born female. My son in his thirties is accepting of the gender woo in his working environment. He shrugs his shoulders as to how it might impact the future of his three-year-old daughter when she goes to school or joins a youth project.

Ironically my husband of 54 years decided to announce to me, his three adult sons and the world that he was 75% woman and had been aware of this for 30 years. He called himself Sophie and said he had a fiancée called Rowena. After a year however, his dresses and accessories have been disposed of. Previously he was a naturist and then pagan. I think he might now be bi-sexual.

The revelation of a seemingly successful 'female-to-male' (trans identifying female) in their thirties in my wider family circle shook me to the core as I had without question accepted their persona of husband, father to two small children and successful businessman. Also within the family is a 12 year-old girl being supported by her mother as non-binary.

To me the most perturbing aspect is that it has taken the women's sport controversy to peak the wider population. I am heartened that women in jail will now mainly be kept safe from abusive males as their presence could only be classed as torture. To me the main concerns should now be women's rape and abuse crisis centres followed by washing, toilet and changing facilities.

Women should be able to congregate without being forced to accept anyone born male in their number. The majority of people under 55 unless immediately impacted seem careless of these issues.

• • • •

Anon

27

I don't call myself non binary anymore

This is hard to say. I identified as non-binary and had several relationships with trans people, and I felt very much at home. I have also at different times described myself as queer, as lesbian and as polysexual. It was the absolute hate for J. K. Rowling that first made me uneasy. It seemed only to be founded in rumour and then the same about the *LGB Alliance*. I was told it was set up with the sole purpose of being a hate group. I came across a stall - They seemed harmless, but I felt wary. Then I watched the conference on YouTube and was really in agreement with everything that was said. I saw Sinead Watson's testimony on Twitter and liked her honesty. I also knew detransitioners but they disappeared from the scene and I lost touch. I can guess why.

     I had joined Twitter and first learned what a TERF was from a trending hashtag which featured trans teens brandishing weapons at the camera and with variously overt or implied threats to kill. These people were unhinged. It seemed to be a hate cult. It has crept into what I used to call my community and not done trans people any favours at all. I now don't call myself non-binary any more and certainly not queer as this has now taken on a darker meaning. I don't want to be associated with this witch hunt of older women or with the predatory capture of young people. People like Jeffrey Marsh make my skin crawl. I have started to feel uneasy in LGBT places. I don't know which of my friends is safe to talk to. I have lost some already. I don't mind losing them as if they are that dumb really is no loss, but I don't want drama. I don't want arguments as they are so extreme. You can't have a discussion. Stonewall's 'no debate' line has destroyed my community from within and without. It's been a hard journey and very sad. "Lord forgive them, they know not what they do."

· · · ·

Anon

28

I felt outrage

I work as a senior clinician in adult mental health.

I was asked to assess an individual who had 'transitioned' from a male to a trans-female. They were continuing to experience clinical depression and anxiety. Within the clinical interview it quickly became apparent that this person was autistic. At the end of the interview I asked what they would want to change about themselves, if anything (to elicit goals for therapy)

The answer was, "to be a girl of course…"

I felt devastated that this person had been led so seriously astray, been mutilated by a surgeon, given hormones and no one had checked out such literal thinking. They had retained all their stereotypically male hobbies and interests.

I felt outraged that such a vulnerable person had been affirmed with no one able to say what they saw for fear of persecution

· · · ·

Anon

29

I was buying 'be kind'

My husband was dubious about trans ideology from the get-go, but I was buying the 'be kind' language. Then somehow, on Twitter I came across a video by Magdalen Berns. She was very ill, near death. I watched one video of hers, then another and another and I felt awful for all the lesbian people in my life and beyond and I just started following GC accounts. I found Glinner, Stella and Sasha, and now I can't shut up about it.

Prisons, sports… but what about the children?

In 2016 before I peaked, I invited someone I didn't know - but from my Jewish community - to my house for a Passover Seder (20 people, religious significance). 'R' showed up fairly drunk, clearly male, put on a shitshow that had us scrambling to keep the evening going (children there).

She demanded I hand over my pills, she needed oestrogen badly. I didn't have any. She was so drunk we had to babysit her while ensuring the service ran well and guests were fed, etc.

After the evening ended, my husband and son drove her and her car home and came back and soon after I rejected her friend requests on Facebook. I figured she was a one-off, a bad actor. But from Twitter, it seems her level of entitlement and assholery even at a religious service in a home was par for the course for some transwomen.

• • • •

Anon

30

Germaine to our argument

In 2018, my sister and I went to a talk by Germaine Greer: *Women for Life on Earth.*

Although Germaine mostly wanted to talk about her purchase and preservation of a forest in Australia there were some questions asking her about her feminism. My sister asked if Germaine thought Caitlyn Jenner should run against female competitors.

I have to admit I didn't really know much about Bruce/Caitlyn Jenner back then. This was the first time I realised that something very disturbing was happening to women; if a man, who merely changed his appearance (or just said he was a woman), was given access to women's sport and then competed 'as a woman', what other women's single-sex spaces were going to be removed?

I've read and seen much more since then about prisons, children, changing rooms, hospitals, etc. but Germaine Greer was the source of my original 'peaking'.

• • • •

Anon

31

TERF journey

How did I start on the path to the gender ideology critical world? It seems like a recent thing, with much of the world just beginning to see the issues that arise when we pretend humans aren't a sexually dimorphic species, but my first hint that there may be a clash between trans identifying people and the LGB community came much earlier. It was 2001.

I was only 20 at the time and out on the gay scene in Glasgow regularly. Midweek drinking sessions were not unheard of for us and this particular Thursday night when I was introduced to this potential flashpoint between the newly emerging 'T' and the old LGB was no different. That night I was out with my brother and his then boyfriend, drinking our way around the merchant city. As closing time approached I suggested we move on to popular LGB nightclub Bennets. I was surprised to get an immediate, "No way, it's crosslink tonight!" type of answers from the people I was with. I was curious and obviously asked what the issue was, to be informed by my brother, "Crosslink is the T night, it's full of straight guys in dresses annoying dykes and growling at us, you don't go there on a Thursday!"

I was slightly baffled, but I accepted that they had been made uncomfortable by this new group who were now being ushered in on a large scale to the gay village. I never gave it much thought for a while after that.

Until 2018 to be exact.

We all now remember the faux outrage and 'anti trans' headlines vomited all over the internet by Pink News after the Pride march in London was blocked from leaving by a small group of brave women, lesbians, trying to raise awareness that the situation in the community had deteriorated massively since the T had become a full time member, under Stonewall's pound sign-filled eye. My ears pricked up. I had heard this before! I was horrified to see Pink News painting this as a bigoted, anti-trans stunt when

I had heard so many years before that heterosexual men had become a problem within LGB spaces. This was NOT new. I dug further. While searching for news footage of the London march I scrolled down the recommended list on YouTube. A video caught my eye and I clicked.

Magdalen Berns filled my phone screen and began talking and that was it. I knew who was on the 'right side of history' and I too began to speak out on social media. The abuse back then was there, but on a smaller scale than I ever imagined it would be just a few years down the line. The full scale dystopian nightmare of the institutional capture as far up as our government and police force, were still waiting to pop up like a demented jack-in-a-box. But pop up it did.

For me it came screaming into my personal life in a very nasty way in 2021.

I was violently raped in June, 2021 by someone I trusted enough to let into my home. I did everything I was 'supposed to do', like see a medic (female, insisted upon by the GP receptionist) and have samples taken. I went to the Rape Crisis website, only to see that they were 'inclusive'. Inclusive for men, that is. They were insisting that trans identified males were women, including the man running Rape Crisis, and seeing his media presence where he expressed much interest in 'orgasms in rape victims'.

I threw up. No way. I couldn't talk to them. They were excluding women whose PTSD couldn't 'be kind' as it doesn't work that way.

Just weeks later I attended Glasgow Green in support of Marion Millar, and my journey to full-blown, taking to the streets TERF was complete.

Enough is enough.

A woman is an adult human female.

• • • •

G. Wilson-Stonestreet, aka 'Ladycultreboot'

32

Grumpy, radical feminist

What brought me to the GC battles: I'm a child sexual abuse survivor, born and raised in Brazil, who was constantly 'educated' by society that women were not oppressed anymore. But I questioned everything, like sex stereotypes, women and men's social roles, and especially why I was sexually abused.

Fast forward to 2011, when I was denied medical assistance for three days while having a miscarriage at 16 weeks. I nearly died, and the negligence and total lack of information about miscarriages had a profound effect on me. Before, I would question and look for answers, but after that I started questioning men in authority, besides looking for evidence. When I got pregnant again, a female friend told me all she knew about obstetric violence and asked for help to raise awareness. I've been an activist for birthing women since 2012. I had no clashes whatsoever with transactivism until 2016, when a 16-year-old girl was gang-raped in Rio de Janeiro by 33 men.

The year before, an Indian female medical student was gang-raped by six men and also impaled, dying from the injuries. I was questioning even more and friends introduced me to feminist theory, to help me to understand why I was sexually abused and why 33 men raped a 16-year-old girl. At the same time, I started to see transactivism in action - at first it was as a 'tolerant' bunch fighting for social justice - and I was ready to embrace it, when some of the same friends told me that women were banned from a Facebook for 'natural gynaecology' because they objected to being reported and cancelled by men in the groups, who were forbidding these women from talking about female issues.

At another point, another story came to my attention, where men who say they are trans went to a feminist conference and were allowed to use the female toilets. After the event, some of these men went to social media to claim that, "Radical feminists' 'synchronized their periods' with the aim to offend the men who say they are trans", and that the female toilets bins were full of "dirty, pongy tampons." I recognised the misogyny in their speech and went deeper on the roots of female oppression, reading all I could on the feminist theory/radical feminism. That's when I fell down the rabbit hole and found out about masculinists, sissy porn, fetishes, paraphilias, autogynephilia, *Big Pharma, Big Tech* and finally peaked for good.

Since then, I started charting female oppression around the world as evidence that not only women are oppressed, but also that female oppression reaches all women on a global scale, regardless of social class, skin colour or even a self-declared 'male gender-identity.'

Since starting my thread on female issues, I also delved into writing about the feminist theory, and in 2020 I self-published a book called *The Grumpy Guide to Radical Feminism*.

• • • •

Andreia Nobre

GALLERY

Gallery 1

Tafod y ddraiges - (The dragoness' tongue)

Manchester - Welsh Women's Rights Network

Gallery 2

Newport - Rally for Jen Swayne

Feb 24 2022

Gallery 3

Bristol - Standing for Women

June 19 2022

Gallery 4

Bristol - Standing for Women

June 19 2022

Gallery 5

Bristol - Standing for Women

June 19 2022

Gallery 6

Bristol - Standing for Women

June 19 2022

Gallery 7

Harry Miller's Victory outside Royal Courts of Justice

February 2020

Newport

Feb 24 2022

Bristol

June 19 2022

Gallery 8

Kara Dansky

At the February 2020 WoLF event, "Fighting the New Misogyny: A Feminist Critique of 'Gender Identity'" at the Seattle Public Library

Kara Dansky

Outside the U.S. Capitol in 2019, speaking out against the redefinition of sex to include 'gender identity' in federal law.

Kara Dansky

Speakers' Corner, Hyde Park, March 2020, International Women's Day.

Transpositions

part II

33

The eve of the war

No one would have believed in the first years of the twenty-first century that the concept of biological sex was being watched keenly and closely by so-called intelligences lesser than man's and yet just as mortal as his own; that as we busied ourselves about our various concerns we were scrutinised and studied, perhaps almost as narrowly as a man with a microscope might scrutinise the transient creatures (or Guardian 'journalists') that swarm and multiply in a drop of water.

With infinite complacency we went to and fro over this globe about our little affairs, serene in our assurance of our empire over reality. It is possible that the infusoria under the microscope do the same. No one gave a thought to the world of 'gender studies' as a source of human danger, or thought of it only to dismiss the idea that any rational person with even a solitary working brain cell assuming it being impossible or improbable.

It is curious to recall some of our mental habits of those departed days. At most terrestrial women and men fancied there might be other people taking seriously gender and queer theory, yet in no way ready to instigate a missionary enterprise on us. Yet across the gulf of society, minds that are to our minds as ours are to those of clownfish - or perhaps gender theorists from Berkeley - intellects minuscule and foul and unsympathetic, regarded this biological reality with envious eyes, and slowly and surely drew their plans against us. And early in the twenty-first century came the great Butleresque disillusionment.

So vain is mankind, and so blinded by her vanity, that no writer, up to the very end of the twentieth century, expressed any idea that intelligent life might have believed that there were not only two sexes in humans and all other creatures, or indeed at all, beyond its earthly level. Nor was it generally understood that the fact that every living human came forth from a woman would ever be denied by a sentient, living man or woman, or staff attorney with a former leading American human rights organisation.

* * * *

The great writer HG Wells himself could not have envisaged a 'science fictional' dystopian narrative as the one in which we now find ourselves. Such a dreadful repudiation of established science as the denial of biological reality, I admit, grates painfully against every fibre of my being, and whatever limited tolerance I had for self-absorbed dogma has long evaporated into the oppressive black hole of Twitter.

The basic fact that there are only two sexes in humans is as accepted by, and embedded into, science as the scientific fact that Evolution occurred over billions of years on this planet giving rise to the varied and wonderful Fauna of this Earth. So much so that it has hardly been mentioned in school biology books for years. One notorious group of religion-infused Evolution-deniers are known as Creationists. A subset of them - the Young Earth Creationists - postulate - no, assert - that the Earth was created by the God of Abraham on a non-geological time scale of thousands of years, rather than the true age of the Earth which on scientific and geological evidence accrued over the past hundred years or so is generally estimated to be, and accepted as, 4.54 billion years. The seventeenth century church leader, James Usher made his now infamous estimate of the age of this planet by 'counting the begats' backwards from the New Testament and concluded that the Earth was created in 4004 BC - or to quote his own words, "The entrance of the night preceding the 23rd day of October... the year before Christ 4004". This is essentially around 6 pm on 22 October 4004 BC, as per the Julian calendar - around tea time. One wonders if it was created before or after a light evening meal of halibut. (This is in fact where the well-known historical quote comes from; 'That halibut was good enough for Jehovah.') This splendidly inept estimate equates to 6,026 years for the age of the Earth. This is wrong by a factor of 753,400. This not insignificant error is equivalent to believing the distance between London and Sydney is only approximately 2.3 metres.

Yet many Young Earth Creationists accept this as fact. *Why?* Because their holy book or their preachers tell them it is true. Displaying such blind acceptance and an egregious lack of critical thinking at this level is cultish behaviour and one should not take this seriously in terms of treating their claims as true. I said one should not take this seriously - sadly though, we are now in a position where we must take a similarly unfounded and bizarre contention as part of a different belief system very seriously indeed. This belief system is gender identity ideology.

Perhaps as the world is becoming less and less religious, certainly in the West, some humans needed to replace religious belief with something equally as mutable. For many credulous or easily-led groups - Bristol University students perhaps - have discovered their own religion and are now playing with the dangerous and insidious internet toy of gender identity ideology. Because what the world really needs a is new religion, many are inhaling deep, long addictive draughts of the fetid breath of genderism.

What is gender identity?

No-one seems willing - or indeed able - to define it adequately, despite laws being made and refashioned around this new and dangerously nebulous concept. Not even Stonewall can - which is very odd as this formerly noble and useful organisation seem intent on pushing it through every letter box and into every government policy and into every work email and into every school book they can.

Gender as a concept. Gender as a soul. Gender as a living thing. Gender as an ephemeral thought in the flimsiest, flakiest, most self-aggrandising yet vulnerable young minds. It is a destructive trend like no other in living memory. It is a contagious fashion and it is a fashionable contagion. It is the new opium of some of the people. It is the living sigh of an 'oppressed' creature.

It has to be said that we may all be affected or disrupted or angered or irritated by its effects on government, high street stores, sport, news reporting and journalism and also The Guardian - but women and girls infinitely more so - and to invasive and insidiously dangerous degrees.

It becomes not an inclusive thing but exclusive. It is the people who refuse to comply that are now seen as the outcasts

- as the pariahs. The generally positive and desirable merits of Diversity and Inclusivity have been taken, twisted and moulded into a social justice tool for controlling others' language, thoughts and actions - and even bodies - under pain of societal disgrace and shame. None of us wish to be seen as prejudiced or as bigots so we may seem willing to comply with these 'inclusive' edicts, for fear of causing public offence and also because most are not well-informed about the difficult and complex issues encompassing gender and self-ID.

In terms of Creationist beliefs I have heard it said, "What harm can their beliefs cause to others? Why not just let them get on with it. Just leave them alone - they are harming no-one," and other such well-meaning but futile platitudes. This is true only up to a point. When Creationism attempts to inform or influence public policy - as it does in many places and situations in the USA - such as in government and schools, then we need to be wary and we need to fight back against ideas and concepts which are set in ideological quicksand.

The same can be said for gender identity ideology. Some of the behaviour borders on religious fervour and has many similarities and parallels with various cults. There are key signs that should send alarms and shudders throughout thinking people everywhere. A cult for example may have attributes such as; shaming its enemies, influencing others by indoctrination, demanding submission, mantras (TWAW! - 'Transwomen are women!' and the less common 'Transmen are men!'), unique, invented language or phraseology, claiming oppression and persecution where little or even none exists, and so on.

There are more similarities, such as a propensity to wrap oneself in flags banded with the most insipid pastel colours imaginable, and a proclivity towards bug-eyed, androgynous Japanese anime-style avatars on Twitter.

The seemingly polite request of, "Why don't you use that person's preferred pronouns?" if adhered to will then become, "Why don't you put your pronouns in your work e-mails? That makes others feel safer and more included." Who can seriously have a problem with such inclusive thought! Yet this step will no doubt eventually morph into, "We, the company, formally but politely request that you include your pronouns in your work e-mails." It is a simple and logical, yet utterly coercive and sinister step to, "You must include your pronouns in your work e-mails or face action from HR."

Pronouns.

Or perhaps, *vanity pronouns* is more apt.

This is where I landed. This is where I entered the fray. It was myself happening upon a You Tube video in early 2017 featuring Canadian clinical psychologist Jordan Peterson speaking with A. W. Peet, a fellow professor at his then University of Toronto, that made my brain twitch into *irritable awareness mode*. The CBC presenter asked Peterson, "Why are you against the use of alternate pronouns?" Peterson's considered and accurate response to this leading question was, "I am against the use of legislation to determine what words that myself and other people are required to utter." The presenter then asked him if he would use alternate pronouns if a student asked him to.

A stony *"No",* was the brutally short answer. I liked Peterson already for his firm and logical stance - and perhaps as he seemed as anti-ideology and as stubborn as I am. The argument grew heated and I became more irritated at his opponent's seemingly inattentive and obliviously self-centred demands for bespoke inclusive language. I could not finish the 17 minute video at that time, I admit. My already gossamer-thin patience soon exhausted by egotistical and coercive linguistic demands on others. This was my very first exposure to the world of gender identity ideology.

And make no mistake, an ideology it is.

No-one will compel me to speak or think in a certain way - no government, no group, no business and certainly no individual. My thoughts will not be controlled or influenced by guilt - caused by 'distress' at my refusing to comply with 'preferred' pronouns or claimed identity.

Think of the *Stroop Test*. This is a specific neuropsychological test wherein one sees a rectangle of words. The words are simple colour names. And the words are coloured in a different colour to that which is named in the word, causing a mismatch. The idea is to read the word that is on the page - 'blue' for example, but at the same time say out loud whatever colour the word is printed in, which may be orange. It is a tricky thing to do quickly, as there are two distinct stimuli entering the brain simultaneously - the reading of the word and the saying out loud of its colour. A similarly confusing effect is happening when you are told to refer to someone with what we may perceive as the 'wrong pronouns'. It can be quite a mental effort to overpower one's natural inclination to use correctly-sexed pronouns - and to keep doing so. That is coercion by guilt. Or legal threat, if you live in Canada...

"Just be nice", they say. Be nice! Why not simply do as they ask? It is simply a matter of courtesy and respect. Other than replying, "Look where that has got us", I would counter by asking this: "What is so nice, courteous and respectful about coercing and requiring others to think and speak and act in way that satisfies another's self-importance?"

Nothing.

No. Thank. You.

As is often said, *he who controls the language, controls the debate.*

What could I do then, as a somewhat helpless individual, to combat this infusion of the new creed? Well, my first reaction is to point and laugh. To use ridicule and humour to demonstrate the absurdities inherent in this and any other damaging doctrine. As long as we have awareness, knowledge and evidence on our side then this is a good approach. No-one gets hurt or harmed by parody or satire. It is not 'literal murder', it is not 'hate speech'. I think the best thing to do at my level - being not in a position of power or influence in any way - is to simply hold a mirror up to what I see as absurd. Use our opponents' own words and thoughts and concepts against them. It can be very effective indeed, if done in a humorous fashion and with care and thought.

My 'targets' are only occasionally individuals, but only those with a loud voice (and a million followers on Twitter, for example) and an erroneous, misguided message, but mainly the ideology itself - the concepts, the language use, the imagery and sheer ludicrous absurdity of it all. As I like to say to Twitter followers after a Photoshop-created parody or satire; 'The material almost writes itself!'

Things are now changing. And soon, perhaps, my 'role' as

somewhat low level, amateur satirist may well be over.

We shall see what the future holds.

*   *   *   *

As I logged onto Twitter, this May the 30th, the year of 2026, the angry, incessant, chanted sound of "TWAW! TMAM!" had ceased. It was, as it were, cut off. The silence came like a thunderclap. The Twitter accounts about me stood faint and dim and unused.

The anime avatars and banners were growing black. All about me the strong growth of science and reason clambered and spread among the ruins of the ideology, writhing to get above me in the dimness. Night, the mother of fear and mystery, was passed. But while that voice sounded the solitude, the desolation, had been endurable; by virtue of it England had still seemed alive, and the sense of life about me had upheld me.

I ventured outside. As I walked alone, the outside world about me gazed at me spectrally. About me my imagination found a thousand noiseless enemies moving away. Terror seized me, a horror of my temerity. In front of me the road became pitchy black as though it was tarred, and I saw a contorted shape lying across the pathway in front of the deserted police station. As this new dawn flourished, as did my courage while the morning stars were still in the sky. I walked on and saw the shape was a pastel-coloured five-banded banner, forlorn and discarded.

At that my heart gave a bound, and I began running along the road. I hurried through the welcome rush of reason that embraced this new, resurgent world.

In another moment I had scrambled up towards the offices of law and order and stood upon its steps. A mighty space it was, with gigantic multi-coloured flags here and there now lay on its grounds, huge mounds of brightly coloured material.

These scattered fragments, remnants of the ideology - dead! - slain by the infectious and healing tenets of reason and science and common sense against which their systems were unprepared; slain as the blue and pink ideology was being slain; slain, after all man's rhetorical devices had failed, by the humblest, noblest thing that he himself, in his wisdom, has put upon this earth.

For so it had come about, as indeed I and many women might have foreseen had not confusion and fear blinded our minds. These germs of ideology have taken toll of humanity since the beginning of things. But by virtue of this natural selection of our kind we have developed resisting power; to no ideology do we succumb without a struggle. For neither do men live nor die in vain.

I again stood staring onto my environs, and my heart lightened gloriously, even as the rising sun struck the world to fire about me with his rays.

The torment was over. Even that day the healing would begin. The survivors of the horror scattered over the country - the thousands who had fled by sea, would begin to return; the pulse of life, growing stronger and stronger, would beat again in the empty streets and pour across the vacant squares. Whatever destruction was done, the hand of the destroyer was stayed.
At the thought I extended my hands towards the sky and began thanking Reason.

With overwhelming force came the thought of myself, of my friends and followers, and the old life of hope and tender helpfulness that had ceased for ever at the start of all this.

And not a pronoun in sight.

• • • •

Al Peters

34

Homesick blues

I suffer from homesickness and hope I can return home someday. My sons who are in their 40s and still live in England say to me, "No Mum, you would hate it here now". For me it is still a joy to visit home due to being with family, seeing familiar and much-missed sights, and the sense of belonging. It is more difficult to relate to the UK when I read the news. It is all so depressing, and I hardly recognise my own country anymore. After 2016 I had to stop reading the UK news so frequently, it was all a big wind-up. Most of us know that UK gutter press are the worst in the world, I never read that shite, but you know, the Daily Telegraph, horrible right-wing perspective on many issues aside was well-written and factual. The Guardian with its leftish perspective, still published factual, reliable investigative reports. Gradually both these papers have become less reliable. I had to stop fuming, read less regularly, and just check up now and again.

On one of my checks, I saw an article about *Women Won't Wheesht*. According to the article a woman had been asked to attend a police interview for the hate-crime of attaching ribbons in the colours of the suffragette movement. This woman had to attend court. *WHAT?* I knew nothing about Transactivists, Stonewall, the erasure of biological sex and the war on women. I had a lot to learn. I began by trying to understand what the different 'Trans' terms meant and moved on to what rights Trans-activists were trying to achieve and how that impinged on women's rights. And, oh my god, it was hard to believe what was happening, and even more unbelievable were the people who were not just allowing it, but encouraging it to happen - 'it' being the acceptance of the hypothesis that Trans-identified males are women.

Female single-sex spaces being disallowed because some males are women. Children allowed medical interventions including double mastectomies and castration because gender is more important than biology and parents concerns dismissed as transphobia. Males allowed in women's prison, yes, even sex-offending, rape-committing type males because they say they are women. Lesbian women not allowed to say they don't want sex with males because some males are women.

Women who say *sex is reality based on biology*, while gender refers to social and cultural labels, getting the sack, abuse, death threats, cancelled, reported to the police, not listened to.

It is hard to watch your country going insane. It is hard to believe political parties, government departments, charities, Amnesty, the police, local councils and more, are supporting this shite while banning words and erasing the connection between women and biology but it is happening.

I am angry.

To the women fighting the above, especially the lesbian women who seem to be a particular target, I love and admire you all.

• • • •

Carol

35

The situation spiralled rapidly

I peaked when my husband of two decades told me he was having gender issues and started to transition in 2015. He had no history of dysphoria but did have underlying mental health issues which were never considered or dealt with. The situation spiralled very rapidly and blew me away, I have never felt so distressed. I was reeling for quite a while on my own as there were and still are no official support groups for women or children who are affected by a father's transition. I was lucky to meet a women who the same thing happened to her just a year before and our ex's were very similar, she put me in contact with an online support group called SPA, which led me to find many more women affected and discovered there was a pattern to the wholly selfish and narcissistic male way, middle aged men behaved during and after transition.

As a mother my primary concern was to protect my young child. The more I researched the topic further and my concerns grew, especially when I got online abuse from a trans rights activist for simply liking tweets about the subject regarding 'watchful waiting' in a medical journal
I looked up hormone blockers and was appalled to read of the NICE side effects and that this prostate cancer drug was being used off-shelf for longer durations on children than it was advised for women with endometriosis who suffered with terrible side effects from its use, leading to legal action in the USA.
The huge failure of journalists to dig deeper though at the BBC and the Guardian to cover this story in real depth at the time, was worrying. In spring 2018 I emailed BBC Panorama and asked them to investigate and speak to experts about the use of blockers on children, which they did in 2019 after many whistle-blowers had spoken up. They highlighted not only the concerns over health but the fact as with adults there was no recorded follow-up or record-keeping after treatment.

The outcomes for children at least, one hopes will be better now due to the Cass Review which found duty of care lacking at the NHS.

However, it is clear most journalists are currently ignoring the *elephant in the room*, and that's the male adults with mental health issues and AGP, many of whom are now TRA activists. There is an ongoing mental health scandal in the UK which is far from over. There are still no dedicated or funded support groups for families affected by adult transition.

Grassroots websites like Trans Widows and Children of Transitioners are raising awareness via sharing experiences. It's notable the woman running the Trans Widows site is demonised and hounded by the same activists and their so-called allies for speaking up even anonymously. She received death threats for speaking to a national newspaper which further highlights the online psychological abuse and continued pressure to try to stop women speaking.

As a single parent, I did not feel safe speaking up as my employers and union have been policy captured, but thanks to others speaking out I now am allowed at least in law to hold my own perspective and not be forced to follow an ideology which is deeply flawed.

. . . .

Anon

36

Overwhelmed with information

It was 2020 and during lockdown I was home with my teenage son, swishing through YouTube videos when a Kellie-Jay Keen (Standing For Women) video came up. I didn't know who she was, or what the subject matter would be, but she was asking that we send 'Happy Birthday' wishes to J. K. Rowling because she needed support. I was intrigued as to why this would be the case and so I Googled 'J. K.' and found her now famous tweet about 'People who menstruate'.

So back on Twitter I went, to follow J. K. and send her some love. I didn't really think anymore about it for a day, as I'd tried Twitter before and not really got on with it. But when I went back for a look, blimey! When people talk about falling down a rabbit hole, that's how it felt. I was overwhelmed with information about the erasure of women's language, spaces, sports, etc, - and the transitioning of children.

I kept on following people and the information just kept coming. I couldn't process it all and struggled to sleep at night. *How come I haven't heard about this before? Is it real?* I felt guilty that I hadn't been taking notice and took a week off social media because I was so stressed.

But then I got angry and realised I could not ignore what was going on. So I began 'educating' myself with more videos by Kellie-Jay, Glinner and Peak Trans and what a steep learning curve it was! I never really took any notice of politics or feminism. Like many women, I thought the war for women's rights had pretty much been won.

Since then I have been busy writing to my MP, signing petitions, filling in surveys and consultations, gone on a protest, bought merchandise and given money to countless crowd-funders, stuck up stickers and flyers, handed out flyers in the street, helped with research, joined the Women's Rights Network and complained many times to the BBC and IPSO. It takes a lot of brain power and sometimes money.

    We shouldn't be having to do this, but at least now the tide is turning and maybe there is light at the end of this nightmare.

• • • •

Anon

37

Incandescent

I wonder what it means to make truly independent choices as a woman, where you don't feel the bustle and heat of objection, the disquiet of annoyance at your stance. I truly understood where women stood in society at the age of 19, thirty-six years ago.

Health is where my journey starts along with the misogynist treatment that this embodies. My husband and I had no idea he had been infected with AIDS through blood products prescribed to treat his haemophilia, and, consequently, so was I. Also learning I was pregnant, I was the one who made the decision to abort my child at a very late stage at 19. Now I am the one that carries the guilt. I should never have had to bear the child I was bluntly advised not to. I was the one who bore the brunt of working four jobs, asking my family for financial support. I was the one writing the letters. I've been left as the one carrying the burden and been ignored for years in the male world of HIV and medicine.

Men who claim to know what it feels like to have an abortion, have periods, be denied being a mother are held in careful regard while women who actually experience these biological events are disregarded and dismissed. I've approached HIV organisations who have not responded to my question regarding the right for biological women to have their own voice. I'm a bigot and a transphobe for wanting to understand what a virus I've carried for all these years is doing to my female body: how co-morbidities affects HIV males and females differently; how it's still affecting me now with the menopause and the female changes our bodies inevitably experience with age. There's no data coming forward as gender is firmly entrenched with HIV organisations for the sake of 'inclusion', when it's actually the exclusion of females.

Incandescent, I fight for female HIV statistics to reflect biological repercussions of a virus that only holds data since antiretrovirals became effective. What happens when men's ' gender identity' data for health impacts data specifically affecting females? This is my main worry and concern. Here we are in 2021 with a society engulfed in gender ideology that it's not only more important as my sex but it's supposedly a label that makes people feel cool, visible, entitled and excuses all types of vile behaviour and bullying - while women are ever less visible, where our female specific medical needs are proudly or glibly secondary, if we are considered at all.

This is why I make my voice heard, put my life of living with AIDS and HIV in the public domain – to protect the daughters and granddaughters of all of us women who bear the impact of gender ideology.

• • • •

Frankie

38

In the name of trans

I knew nothing about gender ideology. I had met (but not been friends with, just acquaintances) males who identified as females and I have no idea if they have had surgeries or just self-identified. They were nice people, just normal, didn't stick out nor want to stick out, just live life quietly.

Then, J. K. Rowling's post on Twitter. The raging responses, the rape/mutilation/death threats were obviously obscene and completely out of proportion to a statement that said, 'Live and let live, but men are not women'.

From that moment I started educating myself, reading every blog, following women on Twitter, learned that 'intersex' is a shunned term and why, that transsexuals are appalled at what is being said *In The Name Of Trans*, and the Scottish government's Stonewalled focus on gender ideology against all else.

. . . .

Shazz

39

I cannot be silent

I don't really want to get Michele Moore into any further hot water with the trans terrorists than she already is, just by caring about the welfare of young people, but she is largely responsible for the moment when I tipped over into *Peak Trans*. It had been building for years, working with a now dear radical feminist friend with whom conversations about my holiday always rapidly became about male violence, and to whom I'd ask constantly if, as a lesbian, I was a bigot for wondering what the 'T' was doing in my acronym, sitting there like a cuckoo. I'd also be asking what a *TERF* was. Constantly.

Then the GRA reforms and *Fair Play for Women* hit my radar, and before I knew it I was at a *WPUK* meeting in Sheffield chaired by Helen Steel and listening to this gentle but impassioned and heartfelt talk by a woman I had never heard of, talking about children being treated as a different sex at school without their parents' knowledge or consent, and I knew at that moment that this was not an issue I could ignore any longer. So, at the age of 56 and a life-long socialist, I became an activist for the first time in my life.

A year after that meeting, I went to the secret meeting of Labour gender critical women at *FiLiA* that had grown out of the private Facebook group my ex-colleague had introduced me to and I became part of the Labour Women's Declaration, one of its founding members and signatories and an ongoing member of the working group. I've nervously addressed a meeting of women members in my local Labour Party, been reported to the Governance and Legal Unit for *Wrong Think* on my local CLP FB group (about which I await a response 2 years later). I have leafletted, had stalls in the city centre, tied ribbons round trees and outside the town hall, dressed the Women of Steel statue in Sheffield, had articles published in the local paper and become a member of a myriad of online forums and groups and taken part in letter writing and other campaigns at local and national level.

I've met my MP to discuss the issue of GRA reform and I know my social media posts have peaked others and raised the issue in their minds making them more able to deal with stuff when it inevitably comes their way. In the process, I've met dozens and dozens of amazing women, many now in real life, but some still only online, and although the campaign for women's sex-based rights is not one I thought we'd ever be fighting, we are - and it is exhausting and like playing *whack-a-mole* daily.

I have never regretted speaking out. I have no job to lose. Others have. But I cannot be silent when I cannot unsee what I've seen or unread what I've read about this gender disease that is infecting our society. It is the hill on which I have chosen to place my mast. It is the defining moment of our time, and I'm proud to be a part of the campaign.

• • • •

Tracey

40

Doing my bit

I have been vaguely aware of the trans debate for a few years, particularly when J. K. Rowling spoke out about it. During lockdown I started reading up about the issue, listening to Kellie Jay Keen, following *ForWomenScotland*, *SexMatters* and subscribing to Glinner's Substack. I work for a Stonewall-captured organisation, although in reality most employees think it's all nonsense.

The thing that really made me realise I needed to do more was the arrest of Marion Millar. It made me want to reach out to other women and men who see the danger to the safety of women and children and freedom of speech in transgender ideology.

I've contributed to several fundraisers, and I've joined a local Gender Critical group. I try to highlight the issues to friends and colleagues where I can. I don't do much compared to others who have been fighting this dangerous ideology for years, but I'm trying to do my bit.

• • • •

Louise

41

Take that purity spiral and...

It feels like I've been aware of the danger gender identity ideology is to women's rights - and indeed to the very fabric of rationality & science - for decades, but it seems to be very recent, much to my shame!

I wasn't very active on Twitter, but followed an account called something like 'Lana del Raids' perhaps in 2017 (now presumably banned). I noticed that she posted some terribly 'unkind' posts that simply baffled me. Why I didn't enquire/wonder what these were about, I can't answer.

I also followed a very sweary, funny, female American mountain biker (I'm a keen, albeit not very good, mountain biker!) My *WTF?* moment came when she tweeted something like, "Rachel, you are a woman and those bigots can f*ck off". On this occasion, for whatever reason I thought I'd look into what this meant. She was, of course, referring to 'Rachel' McKinnon who had just stolen the women's cycling sprint masters in 2018.
It didn't take long to figure out that 'Rachel' was not, of course, a woman. It was full throttle for me from thereon in, with my partner (a medical doctor) repeatedly saying, "No, you must be mistaken..."
I wasn't - and he now knows this. There are not enough *WTAFs* to describe each unhinged revelation of gender identity ideology and I wasn't yet aware of the extent of institutional/policy capture. That still shocks me now.

The next 'big' event - and my 15 minutes of fame - was unmasking Professor Alice Roberts (biologist - apparently - and President of Humanist Society UK) with the simple question, *"I have emailed the Humanist Society... regarding the position on gender identity politics. I would hope the humanists take a scientific approach... Please can you confirm this rational approach"*

Not only did she NOT confirm this, she made comments that led to me saying, "Goodness. Each person can write their own biology? Postmodern biology?"

By this time developmental biologist Emma Hilton (then *Fond of Beetles*) had got wind of this and the thread blew up with asparagus and clownfish! While it was gratifying that the thread gained so much traction, I was nevertheless dismayed that the Humanists and a leading biologist believed in an irrational, unscientific ideology. And, oh the irony, when the 'Professor of Public Engagement in Science' went on a blocking spree (later I believe claiming misogynistic abuse - I saw no such thing on the thread - frustration yes, but nothing remotely abusive or threatening).

My background is social work - mainly child protection - and I have become increasingly concerned at the implications for gender non-conforming children and the horrifying, homophobia in the most extreme form of conversion therapy: 'transing the gay away'.

I was a member of the Labour Party, resigning in November 2020 after Starmer trotted out gender identity, misogynistic nonsense. I am grateful to Maria Maclachlan for hosting a blog on her *Peak Trans* site about this.

Like many women I am politically homeless and quite frankly I dread the possibility of a Labour government or coalition with LibDems as in their current state of ideological capture they would enact the most reactionary, misogynistic policies.

I am also disillusioned with a number of 'left wing' feminists who seem to promote a form of purity politics which I have come to dislike. It has been painful arriving at this point, but seriously they can shove that 'purity spiral' where it won't be seen again.

I am therefore proud to now be involved with a non-party political movement in the 'Women's Rights Network England and Wales' where I am a regional coordinator.

• • • •

Delyth

42

A lifetime of male abuse

I'm not sure how old I was when my brothers started sexually abusing me. I don't know how long it went on. I do remember being forced to perform oral sex on a slew of boys several years older than me, being shown cartoon pornography, being painfully raped by a teenage boy while my brothers watched, drinking urine, and most unfortunately, I remember being penetrated by a dog. I remember not just that it happened, but that feeling still lives in my body. I ran away from my childhood home more than once.

I was a homeless teen when I was preyed on by pimps. I didn't know when I went home with the young attractive couple who shared a blunt with me on a NYC street corner what their intentions for me were. My ID and my few possessions, a nice guitar, a sketchbook, and a couple of changes of clothes, were all taken from me. I was made to sleep on a mattress locked in a basement. My hair, makeup and wardrobe were regularly and meticulously crafted to make me 'sexy'. I felt like a clown. A fake ID was made with my photo which my captors held on to, and I was coerced into performing in a strip club. When I eventually attempted to refuse I was berated and 'given another chance' in another club. This one, I was told, was not nearly as classy.

This time I refused immediately, and was beaten and raped for my insolence. I was 'put on the street' and warned that I was being watched and would be hurt - or worse, as would my family, if I refused or failed to perform. I was not brave enough this time to refuse as quickly as I had before and I was raped, multiple times, for $40 a pop, by all manner of disgusting old men. Eventually I stopped propositioning passers by and began begging, as conspicuously as I could, for help. It must have been more than 60 people who laughed at, ignored, or came on to me, before an older man, the owner of a pizza shop, agreed to help me. Taking me home, he too propositioned me, but thankfully allowed me to refuse, and bought me a train ticket, back to the home I had left originally.

Naturally I ran away again, moving in with an internet 'boyfriend' a couple of states away and a couple of decades older. This too, surprise surprise, was traumatic. I found myself alone on the street again, and farther from home than ever. I began hitch-hiking and was picked up and taken advantage of by too many men to count. I had not yet even turned 18 by the time I began working 'by choice' as a dominatrix in extreme kink circles. I felt that this was the only way I knew how to take care of myself. It commanded higher prices than street prostitution, and provided me the illusion of control. Frequently, I didn't even have to have sex with the men. My specialty ended up being forced feminization, due solely to the extreme popularity of this kink. I became desperately addicted to one substance, then another. I did not escape this world until after I turned 22.

Eventually I got clean and distanced myself from prostitution. It was hard, despite the fact that many, if not most, of the other women and girls I had known from that life were dead already. I still had only ever known a life of dependency on male attention for survival, and I attempted to make the proverbial switch from 'ho to housewife'. I had a child, who became my life. Two years after her birth, her father knocked the pedestal out from under me, becoming extremely abusive not just to me, but to my child as well. In hindsight I see he had always been dishonest and dangerous. Like so many other truths, my mind went to great lengths to hide this from myself.

My saving grace in the family court nightmare we would endure for literally years before our abuser disappeared to make a new family, was the man I had jumped ship to myself. Of course I hadn't learned to stand on my own two feet, and 'needed' someone to provide for us. This new man was kind, docile, a protector and a provider, and respected by the judges who dismissed me without a second thought. He kept us from homelessness, provided us with a lawyer, and after some years, helped me win full custody of my girl, although sadly not before my ex had had the chance to sexually abuse her. This new saviour was also addicted to pornography, lying about it, and treating me as though I was the one with the problem. By far the most decent man I had ever known, and even he jerked off to the personal hell I had lived through most of my life. The very thing that killed so many of my friends from adolescence. The industry that I knew full well was absolute misery for even the most convincing of 'I CHOOSE to do this' women and girls. Girls just like I had been.

I don't know if it was that I was approaching 30 by this point, no longer young and slender and able to 'benefit' from this exploitation, if it was because my pre-frontal cortex had fully matured, if it was because I was finally, for the first time in my life safe enough to admit the truth of it all, or if it was just the straw that broke the camel's back, but it broke, and it broke hard. My mental health deteriorated badly, while everyone I spoke to minimized the harms of pornography use and suggested I learn to live with it, but I could not. I began scouring the internet for other women who felt the same and found them in radical feminism.

Ironically, though I had engaged at great length with autogynephiles for years, before I had known them by that name, it took me a while to figure out why my new role models, these strong anti-sex industry women, seemed opposed to trans identified people. I had known many transexuals in my youth. Urban, homeless, addicted, in prostitution. These were my people. I had not yet made the connection between the fetishistic straight men whose pedophilic *sissification* fantasies I had catered to behind closed doors, and the modern trans movement. Trans people were still, in my mind, old school transexuals; gay men; friends I have known and loved. My internet deep dive pivoted from seeking out other survivors of the sex trade to seeking understanding of this confusing and intriguing divide.

I found very quickly many examples of abuse and boundary violation of women and girls. The cotton ceiling seminar at SFPL, violent creeps like Jessica Yaniv, Karen White, and Dana Rivers; accounts from trans widows and detransitioners; female scholarships, positions and sports opportunities going to biological men: men who were heterosexual and frequently masculine presenting, like Danielle Muscato. I saw women being chastised in PCOS support groups for using the very word 'woman'; fetish subreddits dedicated to masturbating in women's bathrooms, stealing used menstruation products from trash cans, and trap porn, sissy porn, hypno porn, porn everywhere. It was very obvious to me that at the very least, the trans community had some serious predators in it's midst, and shortly thereafter just as obvious that the overwhelming majority of this community didn't WANT to do anything about those predators, and women who pointed them out would be labelled transphobic, bigoted, privileged white-feminism Karens. *TERFS.*

    I have listened now for years to arguments on both sides and I attempt to keep my heart and mind open and full of love, but nothing I have read from either side has convinced me that 'TERFs' are wrong. I have only become more convinced that gender in all its forms, this new iteration included, is sexist homophobic nonsense made to oppress women and benefit men.
    I have seen women speak on this matter kindly, succinctly, eloquently, and truthfully, more so than I will ever be able to, and be demonized, threatened, and attacked for having done so. Like so many of my experiences with extreme misogyny, I turned a blind eye to it, pretended it wasn't there as long as I could, but now that my eyes have been opened...

    I will not look away.

· · · ·

Anon

43

The seven peaks

Peak 1: Staff Inservice/Inset training, 2018

We are seen as being a very diverse and inclusive institution (we have had gender neutral toilets for students since 2016*), and had had a handful of students changing their name/pronouns (though this has increased exponentially in the last two years). The issues with the toilets were ongoing, but generally swept under the carpet in the name of inclusivity and were lumped together with more general toilet issues, and the few students who were declaring themselves as trans were mainly a few girls who tended to have a variety of other pastoral issues.

Like many others, I hadn't really given this too much thought. The staff toilets were still segregated and the toilets were designed along an informal supervision principle to stop bullying and bad behaviour in toilets. The general consensus was that the pupils declaring themselves trans were mostly attention-seeking and struggling with other issues and therefore we should go along with it and not make too much of an issue of name/pronoun changes.

Then we had an Inservice training session. The Senior Manager who organised it had been in touch with Stonewall, who had provided materials that would be presented by a (young, newly-qualified) member of staff with personal experience of having a friend who had transitioned. So far, so good. Staff wanted more information, and Stonewall was the biggest, most famous advocacy group for LGB(T) issues, so the materials were bound to be informative and useful (very unusual for inservice days).

The first 'task' was to get into groups of six or eight and rate each other on the 'Barbie-GI/Joe spectrum'. I looked around at all the clever, well-educated people I worked with, happily judging each other and commenting on clothes, hair cuts and make-up and giving each other a score on the spectrum. In my group, I was asked what I thought. I said I was really uncomfortable judging other peoples' 'gender identity', and even myself, on something that was so clearly based on stereotypes. Another colleague agreed with me and we had a discussion in our group about how flawed the activity was. Some people saw it as a harmless activity to spark discussion, and that it reflected society, but I said I found it offensive that we were somehow grading what being a woman or a man was, and no matter what I wore, I was still as much of a woman wearing make-up and a dress as I was when I was wearing jeans and a sweatshirt.

The rest of the session continued, with the speaker telling us a very emotive story about their friend's journey and how much happier they were now that they had 'transitioned', how it was offensive to assume that this was a phase for people and that we had to accept that people knew deep down what their true gender was. I was struck by the fact this was a story about an adult, and that we work with teenagers, and that changing and exploring your identity is very much a phase that almost every teenager goes through, and has done in various ways for decades. We had further discussions in groups and I was told in no uncertain terms by younger staff that I had to 'educate myself' because my 'position' wasn't right. I and a colleague were slightly bemused by this, but we decided that we should look into this more as our younger colleagues were adamant and also angry with us. So we educated ourselves, and discovered that my gut instinct at that inservice looking at the gender spectrum, that we were being emotionally blackmailed and told that professional experience and knowledge didn't count was completely accurate.

Since then, I seem to peak again very regularly.

Our toilets provision is now being looked at again due to a number of concerns being raised

Peak 2: Germaine Greer, 2019

My colleague asked me if I had heard the furore over Germaine Greer. I hadn't. She explained that Greer had been interviewed on the radio and said that Trans women could never be women, and people were furious with her. I didn't understand, as to me, Greer was correct. Trans women were trans women, who had grown up male, with all the benefits/experiences that brings in terms of social norms and expectations, physical and behavioural traits. It seemed mad and incorrect to me to say that trans women were literally the same as women. I'd heard people say that before, but assumed that people didn't actually mean it. But now the penny was dropping with me that people were now literally meaning that *Trans women were women*.

Dipping more of a toe into this, I discovered that trans women were winning awards for women in business, and Caitlyn Jenner was voted *Woman of the Year*. This didn't seem right or fair, and I was angry that these people were leapfrogging women into these awards.

Peak 3: J. K. Rowling, 2020

By this time, I was on Twitter. J. K. Rowling wrote her tweet about Maya Forstater and then released her essay. It made complete sense to me, and seemed compassionate, considered and sensible. The backlash was astonishing, and I was shocked at how vitriolic, nasty and unreasonable so many so called 'trans allies' were. To respond with such unabashed misogynistic, male pattern behaviour was shocking and I was stunned at the sheer scale of hatred that was directed towards her for saying that sex is real and significant. At this point, I really began to pay a lot more attention, not just to this issue, but because it felt very authoritarian and trying to silence people who don't agree with you. As I explained to a few colleagues, I didn't think you would ever win an argument by sending 'dick pics' to someone telling them to 'eat your lady cock' when they'd raised concerns about male sexualised and abusive behaviour.

Peak 4: Laurel Hubbard and Lia Thomas, 2021-2022

The visual impact of these two mediocre men blatantly taking advantage of well-intended 'inclusive' rules at the expense of women really brought things into sharp focus. The response of the female weightlifting Olympians simply saying nothing and then, *"No thank you"*, in response to questions about Hubbard was inspiring and infuriating in equal measure as they were so dignified in the face of being silenced.

Then came Lia Thomas. I listened to the testimony of the

female competitor's mothers, and it made me cry in anger and frustration at how these young women were having their boundaries eroded, opportunities taken away from them, and told they couldn't speak out. It seemed so authoritarian and misogynistic, and I couldn't believe Thomas was being so supported, encouraged and seen as the victim. Quite astonishing.

Peak 5: The Nolan Podcast, 2021

This was a real eye-opener in terms of the reach and influence of Stonewall. I live in Scotland and I was shocked at how much the Scottish Government has been captured. It made me pay much more attention to what the government in Scotland was trying to do and the activities of feminist groups in Scotland in trying to hold them to account.

I was shocked too, at the interview with Dr David Bell of the Tavistock, and began to look much more closely at the Keira Bell case and the resulting Cass Review. This led me to looking more into the international situation regarding puberty blockers and hormone treatment, and I was horrified that we've been told time and time again that puberty blockers are reversible when clearly this is not the case. I then watched Elaine Miller's clip from the Alloa Women's Festival and her interview with Graham Linehan, which were enlightening, although shocking. I can't believe doctors and the medical profession are allowing this to happen.

Peak 6: Language and Pronouns

I began to notice the changes to women's language and use of pronouns and start to question this far more, especially as there didn't seem to be any equivalent changes to men's language. The BMA's article about bodies with vaginas, plus the changes in NHS wording to include 'chest feeding' and 'front hole', plus using terms like 'menstruators' and 'bleeders' to allegedly be more inclusive seemed incredibly stupid and reactionary to me but also completely dehumanising.

The increased use of pronouns, often presented as *voluntary/no big deal/being kind* also struck me as incredibly regressive. Why do you need to tell people how to talk about you when you're not there? Why do you need to emphasise your gender in a professional setting, where it should be irrelevant (unless you actually do want to remind people of their 'place')?

Your *sexuality/political allegiance/ethnicity* isn't required for you to do your job, so why should your pronouns be needed? Then I realised that it's a 'nudge technique' to make gender ideology slip into daily life and become more accepted, even though we've fought hard for years to try to make gender/sex irrelevant to your ability to do your job, as we have done with other protected characteristics.

Peak 7: Mridal Wadhwa and the Edinburgh Rape Crisis Centre

This peaked me again, as like Thomas and Hubbard, this is firstly a man taking a position that was advertised specifically for a woman. Secondly, the comments made about bigoted women, and those who were raped and that they needed to 'reframe their trauma' were so utterly offensive, it really did highlight how women (even rape victims) are support people in a situation where they should be centred. Women who are raped should be able to set boundaries and not be there as props to affirm trans people.

I could go on. There are so may things that have led me to become ever more incredulous:

- The treatment of women who oppose this (Allison Bailey's hearing, Maya Forstater's case, Kathleen Stock, Jo Phoenix, Milli Hill, Rachel Rooney, etc.)

- The activities of TRAs (in Bristol and Manchester).

- Endless examples of men identifying as trans to get into women's prisons, Wi Spa, Jessica Yaniv, Barbie Kardashian.

- The Scottish Parliament consultations on GRRA Bill (!!!!!)

- The inability of politicians (until recently) to grapple with this issue.

- The willingness of organisations to outsource training unquestioningly and uncritically.

- The huge influence of charities such as Stonewall and Mermaids, which people accept unquestioningly.

- The lack of basic safeguarding when it comes to trans issues in organisations that should know better.

- The behaviour of the police in relation to these issues.

- The lazy approach to being 'inclusive' by making facilities gender neutral/mixed sex, where women are always the losers.

- The attitude of some (men and younger women) who can't or refuse to see how this is misogynistic, ageist and homophobic - with a bit of casual racism thrown in for good measure.

- The undermining of all the good work that has been done of women's issues.

- It all feels very coercive on the part of the Stonewall *et al*, taking advantage of people's naivety and lack of critical thinking.

- How this debate reinforces the old adage of women being *f*ckable, invisible or hysterical*, no matter how we approach it - how we've been ignored, shouted down, silenced and vilified for raising sensible and genuine concerns.

I'm so angry about so much of this, but also at myself for taking my eye off the ball. On the plus side, I do feel a bit braver as time goes on to start challenging and questioning, and it does feel as though the tide may be turning...

• • • •

Anon

44

Finding out

I grew up in the 60s and 70s; I learnt feminism from the Guardian women's page and watched women campaign against sexism. I took a science degree and expected a career; I encouraged my children to follow whatever interests they enjoyed (my daughter now works in scientific research); I thought the direction of travel for feminism was one-way only. I got involved in local issues and became a Liberal Democrat activist.

A colleague transitioned male-to-female, an acquaintance female-to-male, another colleague revealed he cross-dressed; I was cool with all this – I was left-of-centre and progressive. There were niggles though. The transwoman on television making an absurdly caricatured performance of womanhood. Newly-transitioned transwomen instantly getting accolades intended for women. The transwoman colleague getting more favourable treatment than the rest of us.

In 2018, I was working in London, and read the Evening Standard on my way home. One evening, there was a two-page spread about feminism and trans rights. I was astonished to read that feminists like Germaine Greer and Julie Bindel were *no-platformed* at universities: what had happened to freedom of expression? I also learnt the acronym *TERF* for the first time. The article troubled me; I wanted to be progressive and 'on the right side of history', and being a TERF was obviously *A Bad Thing,* but women's rights were important to me. I struggled to reconcile the two until the spring of 2020.

The LGBT group at work published on our intranet, as a BLM/Pride crossover, an article explaining that black transwomen started the Stonewall riots, then the Pride movement. I thought little of it until I discovered from Twitter that this article was untrue. Where do I find out more? I asked. *"Ask Fred Sargeant",* came the reply, "He was there".

So I discovered the article was not only fabricated, but erased the story of Stormé DeLarverie, the African-American lesbian activist, among others. I was now truly peaked. The organisation I work for has integrity and honesty as core principles, and its *raison d'être* is to ensure no-one pulls a 'fast one', but a staff network had published a story which was easily established as being false in all key particulars, and the true version would have been at least equally suitable for the occasion.

So I began to follow radical feminist and gender-critical accounts. I learnt of gender critics losing work, university places and voluntary positions, and saw fury and vitriol poured out onto Joanne Rowling, all for holding reasonable and evidenced opinions. I found out about gender ideology and postmodernism; autogynephilia and the cotton ceiling, children being transed and the anti-science taught in schools. I discovered that the gender stereotypes that I thought had been abandoned in the 70s were more rigidly enforced than ever, and realised that trans rights activism was reasserting the patriarchy with a vengeance.

Learning history, I would sometimes wonder what I'd have done if I'd found myself on the wrong side of a repressive ideology.

I'm finding out.

• • • •

Catherine

45

Like an avalanche

For me, it was like an avalanche. Originally I'd seen the reports surrounding Jonathan Yaniv circa 2019 on Twitter. I started following GC feminists, though GC wasn't a common term then and swiftly learnt of AGP's, the mantra *TWAW*, of DSD's, erasure of the word 'woman', court cases and, my tipping point, puberty blockers.

From then, I read everything I could. The vilification of JKR, Maya *et al* was on another level and I was (still am) happy and determined to financially support relevant court cases anonymously as, fortunately, I am financially stable. I began raising awareness in a small circle and discovered that the average person in the street is utterly clueless about the issue and it's ramifications. I have bored my husband witless recounting the daily updates, but thankfully he 'gets it' at least, and has often backed me up during difficult conversations. I am absolutely determined to get to a protest/march when I can. Work/health is problematic. We have a 14-year-old old son who I made CERTAIN understands the situation lest he encounters gender ideology in school.

I wanted to be part of these voices as I am confident we will look back at this stage in women's history through a comparative eye with those women in history who fought HARD and set the tone. We cannot and WILL not let them down. Neither will we let our children down for we are warriors.

I live for the day when those in the medical setting are held to account for the irreparable damage they have caused.

◦ ◦ ◦ ◦

EO

46

So many rabbit holes

My first experience of all of this was the Gender Recognition Act (GRA) consultation when a friend shared a link on her Facebook page and I thought, "What on earth is this?... *a man can't be a woman."*

I've fought hard for women's rights and been discriminated against for being a mum and being pregnant how very dare they say that. I think I joined Twitter after that and then went down so many rabbit holes, and got crosser and crosser at the incursions in to woman's rights. So many other things; a daughter with a disability who I'm sure wishes she was born in a different body; another daughter with mental health issues on mixed sex acute wards, ended up in prison and the thought there could be men in there with her (Bronzefield, so it could have been).

Since then I've peaked so many times. It's things like the House of Lords debates regarding single sex wards and prisons where these men stand up and pontificate about these poor marginalised men and nothing about the women. I get *soooo* cross, swearing at the screen as they smugly stand there and say things like, *"Well, so a woman gets assaulted - it doesn't mean the process doesn't work."*

• • • •

Helen

47

The price we pay

I woke up when I was told I wasn't allowed to speak about it. It's a simple as that. I didn't notice much until about 2018 but began to follow the discussions on line about the proposed reform to the Gender Recognition Act. I think I tweeted something innocuous like, *"You can't change sex though?"* and immediately a number of people popped up to say I was 'hateful' and they would tell my employer.

As a self-employed sole trader, I wished them luck with that, but it got me thinking. *What is going on here that I may not talk about it?* That any attempt at a reasonable discussion is met with this kind of irrational and over the top response?

So, in common with many of my personality type, on being told I could do not something, I started to do it more and more. I read more, engaged more and became particularly horrified by what was happening to children.

I owe *Transgender Trend* a huge debt of gratitude for providing the information that allowed so many of us to finally wake up. I weaponised my skills at sending annoying emails, and was invited to join *Fair Cop* in June 2019 and the rest – as they say – is history.

At the time of writing – April 2022 – we are beginning to see some really encouraging signs that our efforts have paid off, that many more are waking up and the grip of this harmful and dangerous ideology is loosening.

I am so glad I woke up and I am proud of what we have all achieved. It's taught me some very hard lessons about the fragility of what I thought were well-cemented human rights and that the price of freedom really is eternal vigilance.

But it's a price I am happy to pay.

• • • •

Sarah P

48

The beginning of hell

I am a mum of a 10-year-old girl, living in London.

    2021 - This year was the year when she announced that she hates 'girly-girls', feels like a boy inside and made the statement that she's *a trans boy*. I was given the option of accepting and supporting her with this, and slowly learned that this is exactly what trans folks advise on YouTube.

    The first couple of days I really was supportive but, very quickly, that changed. Having a very analytical mind, once I started to delve into books and hundreds of medically specialised articles, to watch movies and documentaries and listen to detransitioners' stories, it made me realise that it is not something I'd ever support, or encourage.

    Additionally, I have started to scrutinize my daughter's devices to only find out that she has been accessing a lot of explicit content, including porn, along with her friends at sleepovers, but also school peers. In fact, I have learnt that the whole school year label themselves as the letters from LGBTQ. While at sleepovers, from a sort of an anime innocent game called *Gacha Life* it turned into the *Gacha Heat* with explicit LGBTQ content.

    Furthermore, I have learnt that the majority of the parents are not using parental controls on their childrens' devices and I do feel that this will continue to do more damage if not addressed *en masse*.

    I am a masculine mum myself, with a passion for cars, go karts, motorcycles and shooting sports, some of these my daughter also experienced, along with Meccano cars which I also enjoy. My own mum is in the army, therefore transgender/gender ideologies are simply not my values!

    Still, these ideologies have entered my home and have destroyed my small family's peace.

• • • •

A

49

Secretive

I first became aware of trans ideology on Mumsnet, which I turned to after having my second child. I read about it and agreed.

I used to be a Labour Party member and was put onto a published list of TERFs by 'Lily' Madigan, after I posted a petition for women-only shortlists to be for women only. I had to fight to have the list taken down, as I was terrified it would affect my job. I wrote to one of the number of MPs who were editors of the list, including one with whom I had travelled, and campaigned for, in two elections.

He called me a bigot, but he did get the list taken down.

Then I read J. K. Rowling's searing personal account of the violence she had experienced, and her commitment to women's rights. I had similar experiences in my first marriage and her story spoke to me. The appalling way in which she was treated enraged me and I wanted to take action.

I work in a sector for an employer where I cannot be openly gender critical without fearing the response.

I am hugely grateful for people like Marion Millar who have stood up to be counted.

I do what I can as an activist.

• • • •

Elizabeth

50

Women won't wheesht

Like most of Scotland, I missed the first consultation on GRA reform. There had been no letter through my door, no email in my inbox, no billboards inviting me to give my opinion on how men self-declaring their sex would affect my or my daughter's life. I felt it was a particular brand of *sleekit* for the Scottish Government to pretend to have a full and comprehensive set of answers to questions few had known were being posed.

To further learn that the word *Woman* would be redefined in Scotland to include men, for the purposes of the representation of trans-identifying males on Public Boards, was infuriating, but it was also hurtful. It is an act of brutality to dehumanise, and the Scottish Government had dehumanised the women of their country by diminishing what it is to be female.

Stealth has been gender ideology's greatest tool. If women are not informed of what is at stake, how can they defend what *is* at stake?

When it becomes clear your Government isn't even trying to listen to you, since they effectively denied you the chance to speak in the first place, you know you must find your own way to break the silence.

I am hurt for all Women, but I am frightened for one in particular- my own daughter who lives with a disability. At some point, I will not be here to advocate for her. I have a responsibility that stretches beyond my own lifetime. To think that suddenly she might live in a society where her right to privacy and dignity; her right to same-sex care is cast aside for the feelings of men, is overwhelming. I hadn't ever thought I'd live in a society where womens' and girls' boundaries would be dismantled. I suspect even now a fair proportion of Women in Scotland still live under that misapprehension.

That was why I decided to begin the *Women Won't Wheesht* Ribbon campaign. Women needed to know that their rights to single-sex spaces and sex-specific care were in jeopardy. Lockdown restrictions compounded the issues surrounding communication as conventional protest was prohibited. That's when I decided to embark upon a campaign. I decided to wrap ribbons in the colours associated with the Suffragettes around lampposts, fences and trees and post photographs of them on Twitter along with the hashtag *Women Won't Wheesht*. This was in December 2020 and it was an attempt at spreading word of what was happening to our rights from one woman to another through a symbol that echoed the spirit of the Suffragettes. If our voices were not to be heard, then at least they would be 'seen'.

I couldn't have envisaged that so many women across the world would embrace the hashtag or that they would begin tying ribbons of their own.

But I couldn't be more pleased the word woman is now written in ribbon in so many parts of the world.

• • • •

@Dis_critic/Wheeshtcraft

51

I am not going to be quiet

Four years ago I was posting photos of Nicola Sturgeon leading the Pride March in Glasgow. (It's only when it came up in my memories that I noticed all the 'TRANS RIGHTS NOW' placards.)

My sister and I sing - we were the light entertainment at an LBGT performance of *A Midsummer Night's Dream* - Titania was played by a (lovely) great big bloke, a roadie, who was mid transition. (It was a great night, except for bringing my Mammy who couldn't stop snortling every time Titania appeared.)

Other transsexuals I have known have been 100% gay very feminine men- who have gone through hell to get surgery, and I would never dream of referring to them as anything but 'she'. So you could say I was a fully paid-up trans ally.

My adorable niece came out as a lesbian at 15 - no easy thing to do in a rural area - and we've been a safe space for her ever since. She brought two gal pals to our studio for an evening - with firm instructions that they were both 'non binary'. One was clearly a lesbian, the other one chatted up the husband.
My darling niece is now 21 and living in Edinburgh - and there are no lesbian bars left - they are all full of men who think they are lesbians, and think my niece is transphobic for not wanting to have sex with them - which fills me with rage. She told me that there was a new lesbian bar opening - and I had to tell her, it's a Canadian guy, who calls himself a lesbian... (She thinks I'm a bit *Terfy*).

Then there was the talk about Women's sex-based rights at Edinburgh University at which Julie Bindel was attacked by a trans-identifying man, Cathy Brennan. I was totally shocked.

In the following days several things happened. I was chatting in a pub to a pal who knows Brennan. She told me, 'Oh

Cathy was just really angry because she's having trouble getting hormones', which I couldn't get my head around as any sort of excuse.

Then I read Brennan's article in the *Skinny*, advocating violence against women. When my friend, the poet Jenny Lindsay, sent an anodyne tweet to the *Skinny,* along the lines of, 'Guys, seriously, publishing this?' it kicked off two years of complete hell for her. Her career stopped dead. She had death threats - she had to leave Edinburgh - all painfully documented here.

Then, Andy Wightman, a man I admire hugely - I campaigned for him when I was in the (coughs) Green Party - was excoriated by his party - the Scottish Greens - for turning up at the event at all. (As is now well known, eventually he was essentially forced out of the Scottish Greens and absolutely vilified as a 'transphobe' - because he wanted to give women undergoing forensic examination the right to be examined only by another woman.)

Then I read, out of curiosity, the Edinburgh Trans Rights Manifesto - the most batshit piece of lunacy I've ever read (And I was in the Revolutionary Communist Party when I was 18).

It was at this point that I had to ask myself, as a former 'be kind' parroter- who the baddies actually were.

I am a bit late to the party, but hopefully making up for it.

. . . .

Anon wife

52

Good knight

I initially abhorred that anyone could have a problem with any of the good, 'proper' transsexuals we've celebrated our whole lives. I grudgingly listened to my sister-in-law explain what was recently happening underneath it all, then looked into 'self id', considered the abuse of it, and then betting myself I'd find porn categories of men wanking in girls loos 'as a thing'.

It was like lifting the rock and seeing the beasties. Then comes the aggression of the trans activists, realising they were the same men that tried to proudly label themselves as 'incels' until that backfired - the EXACT same language - it's the same guys. Except this time they have figured out what has not only emboldened them, it has made them protected - protected in law - and the naivety of society as a whole, the ignorance of all this has gone as far as empowering them.

The more you look the more you see, and most of it is hidden and unseen from normal people. The more I've tried to shine a light on it, the more friends I've lost. None of it has ANYTHING to do with the trans people I've always known and loved. The exact peak moment, I can't narrow down, but it's a long and ugly process, but born out of a reasonable mind that's willing to hear a debate - a debate that they aggressively want hidden from the general public.

I think, in short, my fabulous and very loving sister-in-law brought it to my attention, and she was the last person I would ever have expected to say there was a problem with trans. But it shocked me, and I obviously had to hear her out.

I had no idea about any of this.

Now I'm terven knight.

• • • •

Anon husband

53

An active voice

I got involved in a group called *Full Time Mothers* about twenty years ago when I had two small children and wasn't working outside the home. The group evolved into the campaign now known as *Mothers at Home Matter*. For a while about ten or twelve years ago I was more active within it, going to the AGMs and working on the newsletter and committee. As well as struggling to choose a more 'media friendly' name for the campaign, we were constantly facing the issue of whether or not our campaign was a feminist one; the group was diverse and included conservative as well as left wing voices, many were resistant to the idea it was a feminist campaign, believing all feminism to be Liberal Feminism and focused on getting women into the workforce and children into childcare.

A group of us who align more with Radical Feminism felt strongly that mothering is a feminist activity and represented the campaign at various feminist events, memorably the *Feminism In London* events held in, I think, 2014/2015. It was at these that I first encountered feminists who couldn't believe we weren't talking about 'parenting' rather than mothering. I, and others, believe that mothering is a physical and emotional role exclusively done by women, people with adult female bodies; not something which defines being a woman; not something all women can or wish to do, but something that only women can do. Campaigning and being on Twitter making these arguments, calling up reports on the disproportionate burden of unpaid work done by women, especially women with children, inevitably brought us up against those lobbying for trans rights who wanted to claim the word 'women' for people with penises.

I have had an active voice in this debate for nearly a decade and have watched with horror as women have been silenced, the concept that 'trans women are women' has taken hold, and Stonewall's orthodoxy has been accepted in so many workplaces.

    I have also had three children go through the secondary school system in that decade and seen huge changes there in what is taught and understood about gender and the mutability of sex. I have huge admiration for the hundreds of women who are visible, and thousands who are more invisible, campaigning and lobbying for women to retain their hard-won rights.

· · · ·

Melanie

54

The awakening

I don't really feel I was peaked, just reawakened from my comfortable complacency.

I suppose I am, what might be politely called, a *Second Wave Feminist*... also known as old! I was a tomboy. I was the first girl at my school to take woodwork instead of cookery classes. I was once the first female at my place of work to wear trousers... unbelievably it was the early 90's.

At university I studied sociology with human biology, so I am fairly confident I know what a woman is. As a classic lefty liberal I was fairly happy with how things were going with women's and LGB rights and I relaxed into early retirement. How would I fill my time? Perhaps give this 'Twitter thing' a try for a bit of fun. I go to a lot of live comedy gigs so I decided to follow comedians and a bit of world news.

Well, it was fun for a while and then Graham Linehan started talking about how womens' rights were being threatened and he was getting viciously attacked for it. I had to start reading more to find out for myself what was going on. So I started to follow a number of Twitter accounts that he was following and reading linked articles and I was honestly shocked. What was this attack on women's rights by so-called 'gender ideology'? I had written my dissertation on advertising in women's magazines and the way advertisers were holding up ideal role models for their respective target audiences. Like any good feminist, I saw these 'role models' as outdated - something to be broken down and I asked myself, "It would be interesting to review the same magazines sometime in the future to see what effects, if any, *The Women's Liberation Movement* has had on the role of the 'ideal' female, wife and mother."

What I discovered was this 'new' gender ideology was *regressive* rather than *progressive*. There was an obsession with the old fashioned masculine/feminine stereotypes and suddenly people were declaring that they were 'born in the wrong body' and could literally change sex. I was dismayed. Just looking back at the music business of the 1970s and 80s shows how accepting everyone was then of how women and men dressed or wore their hair.

In 2018, after lobbying from trans activist groups, the government decided to consult on reforming the Gender Recognition Act of 2004 with a view to introducing a non-assessment/self-identification process for legal gender recognition in England and Wales. I knew the repercussions of this would be far-reaching and would mean an end to women's single-sex spaces such as changing rooms, shelters, rape crisis centres and prisons. I had to oppose this.

From then on I became even more actively involved in what has now become known as a *War on Women*. Of late, however, my biggest concern has become safeguarding children from the gender ideologues. One of the most shocking things is that of parents who take this ideology on board and label their toddlers 'trans' rather than just accepting gender non-conforming behaviour. I should say, if I was peaked by anything, it was pictures of 'packers', which are imitation penises to be inserted in little girls underwear.

The Department for Education needs to take responsibility for some of the materials that are now being embraced by schools - materials that have no basis in science or fact, yet are being taught under the guise of 'inclusivity'. I have been appalled in particular by the rapid rise in teenage girls apparently suffering from gender dysphoria. Due to affirmation-only treatments they have been put on a path that leads to the removal of healthy body parts and lifelong medicalisation. This is a medical scandal being highlighted by the growing numbers of detransitioners. I now have a wonderful little grandson. He loves all colours, he plays with all toys and we will teach him that he can be his true self without being put in a box or having a label or a gender identity. We will teach him there is more than one way to be a girl or a boy and that he is perfect just the way he is. That is the hill I will die on, knowing I am in very good company.

• • • •

Wendy

One thing every day

In 1974, a transsexual came to our university to speak to our women's group. He told us that having transitioned he had discovered he was a lesbian. The reception was frosty, especially from lesbians. I felt sympathy and I accepted him as a woman. I thanked him on behalf of the group and spoke to him afterwards in the bar. I found his flirting had a heterosexual male vibe. I would have liked to have asked him, "Why limit your dating pool to lesbians who are same-sex attracted?"

Our women's group was divided between socialists like myself, who did not identify as feminist, and lesbian feminists. Whilst socialist women like me thought class struggle was primary, the feminists (mostly lesbian) were focused on the primacy of the oppression of women as a sex. I think now it is disappointing that our women's group did not discuss his talk afterwards and consider the implications of this man's views.

In 1994, whilst working as a university lecturer, I and others we were summoned to a departmental meeting. The Dean advised that one of our technicians was going to 'transition' and would be using a separate toilet until he had transitioned and then would use the women's toilets. Women were not consulted. I was polite to him and used the pronoun 'her' when talking about him. But I was worried about gender stereotyping because before his transition I had talked to him about technology and science fiction but after his transition he talked about earnings, handbags and clothing. Maybe he was expressing his true self, but I was not interested in discussing fashion and felt stereotyped by my sex.

I was asked my opinion by colleagues and I said that I had no problem with people living as they wanted but I was concerned about the quality of surgery outcomes (could you really create a neovagina?) and that I was concerned it was irreversible if it didn't improve the person's mental health. My views were seen as 'not accepting of his choices'. It worried me that colleagues were so easily able to dismiss the implications of poor surgery and the possibility of continued mental ill-health. I think we see this same attitude today.

In 2004, the GRA was passed. I didn't see it as a threat as there was such a small number of transsexuals. Some time later I recall signing a petition to allow a dysphoric man who had lived as a woman without a GRC (Gender Recognition Certificate) into the women's estate. He sounded a sensitive person who would not thrive in the male estate, and I realise now I didn't consider the implications for female prisoners.

I became aware of a transsexual in our local gym changing in our open changing room despite there being private cubicles. I asked about this and was advised that they had a GRC. I heard women discussing how they felt about a man in a woman's changing room and noticed they were suppressing their views because they were scared of being called transphobic.

Around 2017, I was invited to go to a political meeting to discuss the inclusion of trans people and I knew the climate had changed so much that the views of women and people with religious objections regarding their privacy would be ignored. Even so I was still sympathetic and I still used the language 'transwoman' and 'she/her' pronouns. But I was worried about the talk of self-id. I felt I would be called transphobic in the meeting if I expressed any reservations about men, who claimed to be women, coming into single sex spaces. I was also worried that transsexual people would try to lead us, even though they did not have a women's experience. I didn't go to the meeting but I did send a reply quoting an article from a transsexual who expressed my reservations.

In 2020 J. K. Rowling was called transphobic. I read her tweets and her essay and was disturbed by the meaninglessness of the phrase *Trans Women are Women* proclaimed so confidently by the young actors who had starred in Harry Potter films. I noticed how difficult it was for people like Stephen King and Margaret Attwood to be nuanced and thought I needed to understand the arguments better. I joined Twitter and followed the arguments.

I talked to my partner who had always advocated strongly for trans rights because he had known dysphoric gay men. He too saw how the debate had changed from acceptance to an ideology that denied the rights of others. We agreed that transitioning children was child abuse, that changing same sex attraction to same gender attraction was deeply homophobic, and that entering women's spaces and speaking for women in political meetings was misogynistic. My daughter is critical of the ideology but fearful of speaking out. She would like to go to university as a mature student and study psychology, but she fears it would not be safe for her to express herself.

I was shocked to see that Marxists, who believe in a material reality, were going along with this ideology. I find myself alienated from the Left as I had known, although I remain committed to the views I have always held on class society. I have become more convinced of the significance of the oppression of women as a sex class. I feel I have a common cause with heterosexuals, gays, lesbians, trans people, conservatives to Marxists - anyone who opposes this regressive, homophobic ideology.

I agree with Helen Joyce. I believe gender ideology is a dangerous ideology that must be defeated. We can not negotiate with proponents of the ideology. So far I have mostly donated money - average donations of £25 - and signed petitions. I would like to do more.

I agree with Filia 2021 - *do one thing every day to make a difference.*

. . . .

Pauline

56

Dinosaurs, and nothing pink

How did I get involved in this toxic mess? Well, the first I really knew anything about trans people was back in 2016 when we had Mermaids come into our workplace to do some training. We are a careers company, so we do a lot of work in schools and with young people.

The training was unremarkable... I was very sympathetic to the cause, but didn't really think too much about it. At the time, my youngest daughter was four and was very much into dinosaurs, and nothing pink - the total opposite of her sister, who had embraced all things 'girl' when she started nursery.

This was me being my liberal self. I'd raised my girls as 'gender-neutrally' as I could - giving them space to choose their own path. But I remember, following the training, that I thought my youngest might be trans; I even remember saying (I am SO ashamed) to her, "You can be a boy if you want". *At the age of four.*

I pretty much forgot about it all then for a couple of years.

I joined Twitter in 2019 to follow the general election, I ended up being one of the #FBPE crowd (FBPE: Follow Back, Pro-European Union), and gained around 6,000 followers. I started seeing a few things that I didn't understand. Everyone hating on Graham Linehan, some things about toilets... I remember posting that I couldn't care less if trans women want to use the ladies - they just want to pee like the rest of us.

Twitter user, *DuncanHenry78* replied to me, and linked his Substack article. I was interested in what was going on, as I felt it may impact my gender non-conforming daughter. I read his article, and that made me look at things differently. Then I looked up Jessica Yaniv - and then the final piece of the puzzle was J. K. Rowling's tweet. I'm not a huge JKR fan - I didn't particularly enjoy Harry Potter (although my eldest was obsessed), but what she said, which was so innocuous, and the reaction to it - had me hooked. Around this time a teaching assistant in my 9-year-old's school, as well as another parent, told her she might actually be a boy. And thank God I was ready. The thought that I may have gone along with this had I not really looked into it, haunts me. I've spoken at length with my (now) 10-year-old, who knows she can dress how she likes, love who she likes - but she will always be female.

I have now lost two Twitter accounts due to 'hateful conduct'. The first for saying, "Lesbians don't have penises", and the most recent for quote-tweeting a Katy Montgomerie comment with the comment, "Crackers". I don't know what the quoted tweet was, but the only word I said was, "Crackers".

I'm now being extremely careful!

• • • •

Anon

57

Back into the ring

I reached peak trans in steps. Initially, the furore over Rowling gained my notice. It struck me as extreme - I mean, *death threats?* So I dug a little. That meant reading her essay to see if she was hateful, transphobic and promoting genocide. All I could think on reading it was, "Hold on... why are people upset about this?" What I read was thoughtful, moderate, caring, and compassionate.

I watched every women's competition in the fields where I'm active (non-sporting TBC) add a clause allowing 'Those who identify as women'. Meanwhile, every organisation or group I looked to for support with my health issues began centring the idea of an 'inner sense of gender'. Groups I accessed for work, and personal interests also fell like dominoes.

I began having discussions with people I knew. I got brush-offs at best; "I don't see how it's a problem", and, "Aren't there bigger issues to focus on?"... and abuse, at worst. The usual, 'TERF', 'hateful', 'unkind', complete with online unfollows and blocks. I cried - it hurt - and I retreated.

I reflected, read and soon realised I couldn't turn away. I couldn't remain quiet when the impact of gender ideology was so vast.

So despite the fear, I stepped back into the ring.

• • • •

Anon

58

Fighting for my lost freedom

It started with Philip 'Pips' Bunce being listed as one of the Top 100 Female Executives in the *2018 FT and HERoes Champions of Women in Business* list.

I worked for a City of London firm and I don't think I had ever seen a woman in the office, or at an evening event, dressed in the manner of 'Pips', with ridiculous lacy confections topped off with hair-clips that wouldn't look out of place on a six-year-old. It was pure costume and it was so offensive. Only a man could dress like that at work and be taken seriously as a 'woman'. Then I watched a video of him speaking and discovered what an underwhelming, inarticulate individual he was, as he proudly told us how 'allies' had corrected colleagues who had 'misgendered' him. And I thought, he's an unimpressive man, using his 'special' identity to get on at work, and I was angry.

Before I knew that men were the most marginalised of all women, I was already interested in women's rights. I was involved with gender balance initiatives at work (back when we thought 'gender' was another word for sex) and co-chaired a women's group. We made good progress in an industry which is notoriously sexist. Personally, I always knew that women could achieve anything, having had parents who brought their daughters up to believe they could be, and do, anything they wanted. I've also known, since my first sighting of Boy George when I was about five years old, that a beautiful man in makeup, with long hair and possibly wearing a dress, is still a man.

Before Bunce, I had known a trans-identified male at work. I liked and respected them, didn't misgender them, didn't even know 'misgendering' was a thing. They were actively campaigning to make my firm a *Stonewall Diversity Champion* - and succeeded. I didn't know then what an awful 'achievement' that was.

In those days, I didn't know that we were supposed to believe that trans-identified persons defy all known science and magically change sex. I just thought we were being nice to them, when we respected their identities.

My anger at Bunce sent me off down internet rabbit holes. I discovered Posie Parker, Magdalen Berns, Helen Joyce, Maya Forstater, J. K. Rowling (rediscovered), Allison Bailey - and also I found out that Graham Linehan, writer of some of my favourite shows, was 'cancelled' for not believing this nonsense.

I learned what AGP meant, that there was a 4,000% increase in teenage girls being referred to the Tavistock clinic, that 'gender' is special category data under GDPR (General Data Protection Regulation). And I've become relatively knowledgeable about the provisions of the Equality Act.

I am so proud of Britain and that we are leading the fightback. I live in *Boudicca country* and her speech 2,000 years ago inspires me today -

"We British are used to women commanders in war... But I am not fighting for my kingdom and wealth now. I am fighting as an ordinary person for my lost freedom, my bruised body, and my outraged daughters... You will win this battle, or perish. That is what I, a woman, plan to do! Let the men live in slavery if they will."

• • • •

Anon

59

Every single thing makes a difference

For me it was gradual enough, so I don't really remember anything specific. I didn't have one big 'peak' moment. I was aware of a potential issue for a while, and then it was the GRA consultation where I really got concerned at the concept of Self ID - the idea of the government creating a legal fiction by effectively lying about someone's sex on a birth certificate. Until then the issue seemed like a concern but one that was (hopefully) manageable. But Self ID would have meant a major change that would be hard to undo.

And so that was when I first actually *did* something. I was aware of *Fair Play For Women* through a friend of a friend (through a Facebook group actually), and I joined their leafleting campaign during the GRA Consultation in 2018. I hadn't done anything like it before, and in all honesty it was the scariest thing I've ever done in my life.

On the first weekend of leafleting, I remember getting ready to leave the house to go and meet three other women. My heart was thumping I was so nervous. We'd never met each other before, but that's not why I was nervous. We had no idea what to expect; would people shout at us? Call the police on us? Get violent? We had all these contingency plans about what we would do if we got attacked, how we would handle it, where we would go if we needed to get away and meet up afterwards.

None of those contingency plans were needed. Almost everyone we spoke to was horrified that the government was planning to make such a major change with so little public awareness, and almost everyone agreed with us. I went out leafleting multiple times in multiple different places, in the local area during that summer with various different groups of women - none of whom I had met before and all of whom were lovely and inspiring in equal measure. And it was the same every time - almost everyone agreed with us. And almost everyone who disagreed with us was polite about it. It was nothing like talking about it online.

I began posting about it on my Facebook page during this time too. Friends sent me links to stories about trans kids to try and change my mind, or told me that, "Actually some women do have penises", or they just simply told me to, "Stop talking", and/or 'unfriended' me. When I commented on public posts strangers came onto my page to call me a hateful bigot. Then I had a message from a friend who hadn't seen the issues at first but said my posts had helped her realise why there was a concern. I hadn't realised she'd even seen anything I'd posted; she hadn't interacted with any of it. It made me realise that it all counts, it all helps, every single thing makes a difference, whether you realise it at the time or not.

My most abiding memory of going out leafleting with *Fair Play For Women* is when someone who'd been speaking to the other leafleters came over to me and the woman I was with specifically to tell us, "Thank you for giving up your Saturday to let people know about this. I had no idea and I'm really concerned about the implications for survivors of sexual assault."

She told us how she was going to write to her MP and talk to her friends, but it's that 'Thank You' that really sticks with me - the fact she came over to us just to say that after speaking to the other women.

It was the scariest thing I've ever done, and I'm so glad I did it.

Courage calls to courage.

•   •   •   •

Tracy Duckett

60

Where does this come from?

I guess the question that keeps coming up is, if my daughter is not suffering from significant emotional distress as many ROGD (Rapid-Onset Gender Dysphoria) teens seem to; if her family is intact, loving and functional, if she's not a lesbian or on the autism spectrum, then where does this come from?

She has never just gone along with the crowd. She has always been stubborn and strong. Her confidence and resilience used to floor me. When she was little, I'd say to her (only half-joking), "I want to be like you when I grow up."

But she does have ADD - Attention deficit disorder. She practically had to beg me to get her evaluated when she was in ninth grade back when she was a lesbian, before she identified as a gay man.

My stance until then was, *"You wish"*. You focus for hours on things you enjoy, but when it comes to school work, you don't care. What worried me wasn't a looming executive functioning impairment, but something more along the lines of psychopathy. As in, doesn't it bother you when you don't hand in your work? Don't you care that you're getting zeros? Don't you want to amount to something one day?

But she did care. She was just paralyzed, via a labyrinthine, illogical, perfectionist route. And she did have executive functioning issues. And now she has *Adderall*. Which helps significantly, I admit. She was overjoyed upon learning her diagnosis and even more so when she received meds. She couldn't text her friends the good news fast enough.

Which brings me to 'oppression points', a term I got from Arielle Scarcella during my still-ongoing exploration of the brain-melting trans-teen-iverse.

My daughter's ADD diagnosis and non-binary/transmasc identity give her major oppression points. Now that she's no longer a lesbian, it doesn't serve her to be 'cishet', thus transmasc is her new flag. At least that's my Gen-X hot take.

She boasts these attributes on her Twitter bio and I wonder how the very things people used to keep private they now proudly wear on their social media sleeves. That was one of my first inklings that none of this was real - back in sixth grade when she was pansexual. It's the inverse of protesting too much. The lady doth proclaim too much?

As her mom, my hunch is that the root of her trans identity is her simple unwillingness to ever be basic. She was never interested in the popular kids. Run-of-the-mill white girls did nothing for her even though at first glance she was one herself. From the very start her besties included a sweet little bow-topped angel with Down Syndrome and the emotionally fragile daughter of an active alcoholic. That fragile daughter is now a fragile son, with a testosterone-deepened voice and moustache. There's another teenage girl on cross-sex hormones at the high school that I know of, plus a bevy of girls (and some boys) who employ name changes and divergent pronouns. The angel doesn't live around here anymore.

In other words, in our liberal community, a glittery new kind of basic has arrived. Will my anything but basic daughter see this hypocrisy one day? Will she bravely let one sliver of doubt in - and examine it - before she does something irreparable?

And that's my biggest fear. And that's what this post and all my writing here is about. It's a prayer to a god I don't believe in that my daughter's trans-religion will implode and disintegrate, a hope that she will emerge a survivor and not a casualty. It's a therapeutic writing workshop for a mom who can never quite relax while her daughter considers 'just hormones and stuff' a viable, healthy approach to an imaginary orientation.

• • • •

Anon

A bunch of aggressive lunatics

When J. K. Rowling backed Maya Forstater in 2019 with a tweet, I saw the *Trans Taliban* in action for the first time. It was odd. I just couldn't believe it. What did I see there all of a sudden? Not a trace of sanity or decency. On the contrary. A bunch of aggressive lunatics.

It got worse and worse the more I researched the whole thing. Trans is not what it looks like on the surface.

When this destructive cult completely took over Reddit in early 2020, I decided I had to fight back.

• • • •

Cycledance

Staff diversity

Our severely learning-disabled sixteen year-old daughter, Helen (not her real name), is entirely dependent on others for intimate care. Nearly two years ago, her special school sent round a new intimate care policy, which had been ratified by its governing body:

> *"A decision has been made to remove cross-gender consent from the personal and intimate care policy, which is in line with legislation and guidance relating to equality and diversity".*

In other words, same-sex intimate care had now become *cross-gender* intimate care, a change of policy that would allow male members of staff to take Helen to the loo, one-to-one, behind a closed door. As her parents, our reaction was initially disbelief, followed by outrage, and a determination that this policy change should be reversed.

As Helen's parents, it took us a while to realise the importance of sex-based rights for both her, and for girls and women like her. These rights are under threat. These are the girls and women whose severe disabilities mean that nearly every aspect of their days and lives is planned for them, and done to them. They have no mental capacity (they are fully reliant on others to take decisions in their best interests).

They have no voice.

Their disabilities leave them with no sense of 'stranger-danger'. They are unable to tell anyone if they have been flashed, groped, or raped. They are unable to advocate for themselves or draw attention to their vulnerability through social media such as Twitter.

They are entirely dependent on others, twenty-four hours a

day, seven days a week.

Their threatened rights include:

- The right to have women-only care staff dealing with intimate care, helping use the loo and manage menstruation.
- The right to go to a women's clothes shop, changing room, or bra-fitting service, and for there to be only women present.
- The right not to be seen naked by or see naked men in swimming pool changing rooms (Helen loves swimming).

Obviously, nobody could imagine that male staff would be thought routinely eligible for roles providing intimate care to severely learning-disabled girls, right?

Wrong.

* *

How a journey of awareness began

After we received the school's new policy, allowing male members of staff to be responsible for Helen's intimate care, we contacted the school to question the change. We were told that the new policy had been agreed, *"After seeking advice from our HR Department, the CIPD (Chartered Institute of Personnel and Development) and the partner schools we work alongside. We have also used our Local Authority's template for writing the policy."*

We persisted and sought our own informal advice. Helen's school also sought theirs, this time from a lawyer: *"To ensure that we are doing the absolute best for our pupils without discriminating against any of our staff team."*

This lawyer did indeed tell them that the policy had to be changed back to same-sex intimate care, to comply with the requirements of the Equality Act (2010). However, during these discussions the view was expressed that the law was outdated and against majority opinion. We ended up in a situation where it was agreed that Helen would receive same-sex intimate care, but this was because of parental preference. In other words, Helen's intrinsic and necessary rights to safeguarding and dignity were now conditional on others' permission, on us. There is no doubt in our minds that a priority for the school was to be able to appease, to be able tell the staff, the parents have insisted on it.

    This was the starting point of our journey: that a special school, with all its expertise and experience of teaching and supporting girls with severe learning disabilities felt justified in tossing away Helen's rights in order to celebrate staff diversity.

• • • •

Anon

63

I googled Susie Green

In June 2020, my 14-year-old took me by complete surprise and told me they were the opposite sex: my life screeched to a halt!

Being involved in fandom, tumblr, AO3 etc (no, it's not just for young girls) I was WELL-VERSED in how things were supposed to proceed and the right things to do and what words to use. I knew loads of non-binary, trans and queer people and had a full set of woke friends. I knew who the transphobes and 'TERFS' were, thank you very much. I knew JKR was the worst of the lot and most importantly I knew the sacred mantra, 'Trans women are women'!

My kid said they had always been this way but that simply wasn't true, they had never been like that, not a single sign of it, yet I was being told very clearly they were, without doubt, *trans*. It all felt instinctively wrong and my partner and I were terrified. We couldn't sleep, and we couldn't stop worrying about our child's announcement - not because of 'transphobia' but because we knew it wasn't true.

I joined the Mermaids Parents Forum (of course) but this is where things turned for me. I saw stories not just similar to mine but EXACTLY the same: my teen's words quoted by other parents, four or five new ones per day, every day - I watched it unfold in real-time and...

It. Was. Shocking!

So many parents had kids with ADHD and ASD, nearly all of them had depression or eating disorders, self-harming, suicide threats, past trauma or sexual assault or often, as in our case, been alone with the internet during lockdown having started puberty earlier than their friends.

Mermaids' forum included staff, volunteers and the CEO, Susie Green. There were regular posts by Green with petitions and letter templates to send to MPs, etc, with pre-filled objections to whatever the latest 'anti-trans' scare was. We were all advised to change our kid's names, pronouns, clothes, get on the waiting list at a gender clinic or use the online prescription services of the now disgraced GenderGP to get blockers AS SOON AS HUMANLY POSSIBLE because otherwise our children would harm themselves!

There were some very, very eager contributors on there, some had children who hadn't even come out as trans but the parents were 'expecting it' - even though they sounded completely normal. Others boasted at *just how trans* their kid was, their 'top surgery' etc, or how much they hated a certain gender stereotype (extra proof of trans) or how they helped their daughters get binders or their sons to shave their legs. They were not terrified like me, they were CELEBRATING!

I had discussions in private with parents who shared my concerns, too scared to post doubts - we'd seen what happened when you did. It was all affirmation, all the time but I was genuinely surprised, I'd assumed that this children's charity would be open to new research, compiling data from all these parents, taking about psychotherapy, and *hmmm...* maybe the explosion of new cases and the possibility these children might be mistaken at least some of them - maybe even just one of them and perhaps look into the phenomenon of all these same types of kids, the autism link, the internet/social media link, the lack of evidence, the possibility of side effects from blockers or HRT?!

I Googled Susie Green.

She'd taken her son to the US to be in the first group of children to be given the experimental treatment of puberty blockers, then started him on oestrogen when he was 13 years-old. She took him to Thailand where he received genital surgery on his 16th birthday to remove his testicles and penis. The penis was too small to be inverted due to the use of puberty blockers/oestrogen. *Jackie Green* then became the youngest person in the world to have a sex change.
I could see that this mother's decision taken on her child's behalf meant that it would be extremely unlikely she could ever be neutral or even slightly questioning about 'transgender' kids.

It was now clear what was happening to all those other affirming parents, and that all was not well. My partner and I started our ongoing study of surveys, research, interviews, theories and podcasts to find out everything we possibly could about gender dysphoria in teenagers. *Gender: A Wider Lens* podcast was very informative with some very revealing interviews from experts in this field.

The more information I found, the more I could see the truth behind the pale blue, white and pink curtain.

The actual detransitioners, the whistleblowers, Big Pharma, the lobbying, the funding, the profits, the bullying and lying, the AGP agenda, the war on women and their sports - their identity - their spaces - their awards - their everything, the homophobia, the 'queer' issues, the prisons and abuse, the real suicide and murder facts.

I also discovered the link between game avatars, viewing online porn too young and the brain's mirror neurons, also the effect of isolation (lockdown) on teenagers who start puberty before their friends. The affirming (often grooming) echo chambers of Reddit and TicToc, social contagion...

Despite my previous 'woke ally' position we never affirmed, never changed pronouns and we also found a very experienced, non-affirming therapist. After a year of talk therapy my teen no longer identifies as trans and no longer wants hormones, they are happier, more open and thriving.

I read JKR's essay over and over and still can't see the hate or transphobia that my friends are still convinced it's full of but then their children haven't slapped them hard across the face with the trans flag yet.

• • • •

Anon

TWEET SECTION

Tweet section

This section contains many of the individual Tweets and shorter comments made by people replying to the request for 'Peaking stories'.

---

dvypctr
Aug 13

I was unwittingly in a Twitter bubble ("TWAW! SWIW!" etc) not knowing the first thing about what such TRA bibble was in response to. I assumed they actually were oppressed, which is what people in a Twitter bubble like that do. Endless clicktivism.

My wife had clearer views that challenged mine. She pointed out stickers saying Adult Human Female aren't just people being "mean". I began looking into it and shortly afterwards heard Stock v Hines on Woman's Hour.

That was that. I understood.

Fletcher S. Aude
Aug 13

Katie Herzog 4 years ago on lesbian erasure. It's not that I like lesbians, I don't, or at least not any more or less than i like anybody else, I just really hate erasure.

Ana
Aug 14

Mine is really just one word: **Yaniv.**

I tweeted about Yaniv being in the wrong in 2019, beardy wokebro called me a "terf". Have peaked a few people in turn

Lucy Burgoyne
Aug 13

With me it was so gradual that I can't really point to anything in particular. I never believed TWAW or that Non Binary is a real thing but I would have used they/them for a Non Binary & she/her for a TW at one time, that ship sailed long ago though. I'm hardcore these days.

TheVikingDane
Aug 14

I opened my Twitter account the day @BramhamAlex
 got attacked for wearing LGBA attire. I was horrified and wrote a Tweet about it. Then a lesbian responded saying welcome to the battle. I had no idea but wasn't going to ignore women who speak out. I now do what I can to help.

Chris/shortforChristian
Aug 14

I saw this. I had no skin in the game and didn't really know what the debate was all about. The video shocked me. It's why I, too, have joined the side of realists, scientists and empiricists against the cult and gnosticism that is gender ideology and TRA.

Annie Bishop LLB Hons, Phd in making a fuss
Aug 13

I peaked a few years ago realising that the majority of Tims do not have surgery & are white male and stale it's a fetish and the majority of Tiws are young, female and start early having surgical reassignment etc Then there was all the Hoohana about predators in prison

Gillian KPSS #KeenNotMean
Aug 13

My peaking moment was watching the video footage of Maria MacLachlan being punched to the ground by that young man calling himself Tara. She was a woman of my age going about her own business and that happened to her. Then the court wanted her to call him by female pronouns ...

Interested Observer
Aug 14

Well for me it started with a sky news discussion about censorship of a billboard with the words adult human female on it. It snowballed from there to Yaniv wanting females (often immigrants) to wax male genitalia as if it was female ... Maria then Kate Scottow etc

---

Dignity, comfort & safety - Single sex spaces
Aug 14

I remember in 2019 sending outside the gender neutral toilets in the Hippodrome Theatre reassuring three older women that men using urinals while little girls were walking past to use the cubicals was indeed wrong. One of them was crying with distress.
I felt sick and angry.

Mintypig.WOMAN
Aug 14

I didn't realise what was happening until I followed people on Twitter in around 2018/19 who were being labelled "evil" and "hateful" for- stating sex is important and gender should not be substituted for this- women and girls need their own spaces- holistic healthcare matters.

blackadderbob101
Aug 14

Yaniv. Was already interested in gendered toys/kids clothes issue, which led to discovering the full horror or gender ideology.

Could Be Ewe
Aug 14

BBC Nolan Investigates Stonewall podcast. I couldn't believe what I was hearing. Being called a RW bigot when I spent my 80s in London clubs where everyone looked tranzy and no one gave a shit, but the Ladies was for us and just a few unassuming blokes fixing their makeup.

---

aletheia
Aug 14

A few things together.
1 G Greer 'cocks in frocks' discourse.
2 J Bindel attacked by TiM.
3 Women's Place etc 'hate groups' claims.
4 pitching LGB v women.
5 Lily Madigan scandal.
6 SNP v Alba row.
(but esp Lily Madigan).

Fell into place from there.

QueenOfSons
Aug 13

I was browsing Twitter looking at the insane USA politics of 2019... found some cool accounts, and one day the one account led me to @archer_rs. And HE in turn, one day retweeded Richard Dawkins' comments on Dr Debra Soh and JKR. I have never looked back.

Pigeon Ponders
Aug 13

Mumsnet did it. A thread about Bunce and men taking women's awards and board places. Once I saw what was happening I couldn't go back.

#IJKR
Aug 14

Many things peaked me over what felt like a short space of time. Philip Bunce, 'Rachel' McKinnon, Posie Parker wiping the floor with Harrop on a news channel, McKinnon openly and gleefully celebrating the death of Magdelen Burns and I saw the complete and utter hatred soon and it's ok because the next generations are already on board - this last bit was bragged about by someone with close links to Mermaids. Then I learned about Keira Bell harmed but irreversibly physically too some transpeople and TRAs have for women. Then I found out how many institutions had been captured by Stonewall and Stonewall Law so that we can't trust news outlets or regulators anymore. The capture of schools and the gloating that people who are GC are old and will die off

---

Harryk
Aug 13

I was out of touch living a quiet married life.
 then I saw the same sex attraction is Transphobic sticker somewhere.
I got confused then angry . That sticker made me do my own research.   That was less then a year ago.

Woman
Aug 14

I discovered @janeclarejones and @elizamondegreen. Brilliant articulation of what I had felt about genderism but struggled to pin down. They laid it bare with logic and rationality (and character!).

WestideWitch
Aug 14

Safeguarding children
I've dealt with enough sex offenders to know that some TiM's are perverts in women's clothing. Grooming in plain sight. Sex offences rising rapidly. The access to children readily at hand. Sexual abuse ruins lives forever.

Galaxygal12
Aug 14

I saw someone wearing a shirt with - some women have a penis get over it - written on the front. Not interesting or funny but it made me pause and think about what was happening around me and the fact that I didn't want to get over it I wanted to contest it.

TERRY STEVENSKPSS #MD-ANT
Aug 13

My origin story is simple, saw tweets from, must have been For Women Scotland, about toilets in schools being turned gender neutral, and the girl guides. Had feminist friends since late 70's, the days of spare rib etc. so was aware of FGM etc. guess I'm just an unreconstructed lefty.

Christopher Banana
Aug 14

I wasn't even aware of this whole trans thing, being genuinely friendly with whoever come up to me, including some Trans twitter users while genuinely angry of justice with funky news of trans community about their weird kinks and idea about women.

Then genuinely friendly twitter folks showed up the next day bombarding me with how disappointed they are with me, and since then I knew, this being kind and open thing is a one way talk, only yes and yes. And I am not a yes person.

Lexi Hector
Aug 14

Mumsnet. Spartacus thread. Posters being banned for saying transwomen are men. 2016, I think.

Nun of Your Business
Aug 14

Seeing men's sex crimes recorded as women's. Pedophile men 'transing' to gain access to children.

Men abruptly 'transing' when arrested & the Justice system accepting it thoroughly & unquestioningly, even if the men made no attempt to even look female.

Women of the World
Aug 14

Came across an article about Yaniv and from there went down the rabbit hole. I went from considering myself a liberal feminist to being a radical feminist. Women truly are amazing.

Anon
Aug 14

Off my own bat, I introduced myself using "she/her" in a Facebook group. I stared at my post for hours, not understanding what was wrong. Then I realised- I had zero idea why I thought that was the right thing to do. Cue a deep dive across platforms and views. I landed here.

Heather Sharp
Aug 14

Watching trans Rachel McKinnon (now Veronica Ivy) winning the 35-44-age sprint at the UCI Women's Masters Track World Championship, LA 2018, denying the second-place woman here becoming world champion because of him. The arrogant, entitled cheat won again in 2019.

Morphalina
Aug 14

The Lindsay Shepherd recording led me to Jordan Peterson to Triggernometry to Posie Parker then the Scottish GRA reform. I considered myself fairly up to date on Scottish politics yet had no idea this was happening.

M Logie
Aug 14

the trans boys at the school I worked at turned out to be autistic and read H Joyce's Trans and wondered what the hell we were doing to kids.

Knitman/Colin/Gay not Q word
Aug 14

As a gay man I recognise that this ridiculous TRA nonsense is dangerous to science, bio women and male and female homosexuals or bisexuals because by denying biological sex all of us are denied. I am also naturally anti fascist and authoritarianism.

Kathryn England
Aug 14

Joined Twitter 2018 and saw Graham Linehan as a suggestion to follow. Always loved his wit but was completely unprepared and bewildered by what I saw. Tried to understand and engage with TRA accounts - took me a long time to realise that was pointless.

Helen
Aug 14

I was blissfully unaware until a Mumsnet thread on M&S changing rooms policy did it. My daughter had been the victim of voyeurism in another shop's unisex changing room. Once I learned about all the High Street stores obeying Stonewall orders, I was all in.

Ellie
Aug 15

Seen a few snippets in the media, but it was @sharrond62 & @Martina after I watched a documentary they did on tv after they'd been catapulted into the firing line.

Joe MacVeigh
Nov 01

Magdalen Burns and two other brilliant women.
Lucy Masoud, an old friend of mine and Sian Griffiths who led from the front on women's issues in the London Fire Brigade. Check her out.

Dalziel Kern
Aug 15

It was in late 2017 reading about the Lily Madigan & Aimee Challenor affairs. One young man arrogating womens' positions, names, and influence is bad enough, but two looked liked a bandwagon.

So I began delving and following GC accounts on Twitter etc.

La'Terflon.
Aug 15

Alex Drummond saying he brought out the inner lesbian in his partner. Lots of young lesbians wanting to be men. Trans inclusiveness being more important than women's safety, spoiling mich fest. Now Hampstead women's pond. Women being sexually assaulted in a single sex hospital ward and in prison. The press just ignoring concerns about women and girls safety. Being transphobic for not accepting cock.... Stonewall have a lot to answer for. Gay kids being convinced to take puberty blockers.

WomanSayingNo
Aug 15

For me, it was the treatment of @jk_rowling that initially piqued my interest, but I was shocked at how quickly I became gripped. I think, mainly it's because I'm a mum of a 12yr old girl but I was also remembering things I'd put to the back of my mind....
Such as having severe anorexia and being so body conscious that I would wait until the changing rooms were empty before undressing. Or the times I flooded (period) everywhere and had to clean up. But, I was also remembering a sexual assault (not rape) that happened in a toilet...
At the time, I laughed it off as 'men will be men', but the thought of men being able to use women's spaces, without challenge, triggered something in me. This realisation is what peaked me but it's the thought of my daughter having no control over her spaces is what motivates me

Synthmatrix
Aug 15

The infamous JKR tweet & I saw Joanna Cherry in support. As a Remainer, she was already a hero to me. Any doubts I may have had about whether this was the right side, melted away. From there it was just about gathering evidence. When they came for biology, it was all out war.

Sensible Macavity
Aug 18

I was on the side of trans rights etc believing at the time I was trans but the arguments being used were indefensible when you have men with beards and no intention of 'transitioning' calling themselves women and lesbians. Demanding that women must give up their privacy and dignity to allow these men into their spaces. You are not allowed to question their believes no matter how crazy the claim is and I just couldn't be part of a lie that impinged on free speech and women's rights.

Liz Respect My Sex If You Want My X
Aug 20

I saw a young male made Women's Officer in a constituency Labour Party. A member since my 17th birthday and lifelong activist, I challenged this gently online. The man put my details on a list labelled 'TERF bigots' and some women on the list were kicked out of the Party.

I asked one of the MPs who was a moderator of the list to take my name off and he refused. I contacted some of the other women on the list via Facebook and found some wonderful friends. I am now one of the leaders of the Women's Rights Network - so cheers, Liam and Wes!

---

e n d

Transpositions

part III

She

She was not gender nonconforming.
She was not a girly-girl.
She was not a tomboy.
She was an ordinary girl.
She was very much loved.

She was smart.
She loved to read.
She loved her American Girl dolls.
She played soccer.
She played the violin.
She was very much loved.

She was kind and helpful.
She was a good friend.
She called her mother, mommy—even as a teen.
She was a firstborn.
She was very much loved.

She had a favourite striped dress.
She had bright brown eyes.
She liked to visit the mall with her friends.
She loved to bake.
She was very much loved.

She became interested in animal welfare.
She became a vegetarian.
She asked permission to date a boy at age thirteen.
She purchased bras from Victoria's Secret.
She began to spend more time on her computer.
She was very much loved.

She was bullied on social media by a boy.
She dreamed of winning a concerto competition.
She said she would wear a formal blue gown if she won.

She enrolled in a competitive honours program.
She received a smartphone on her birthday.
She was very much loved.

She came out as lesbian in high school.
She helped to form the GSA at her school.
She uncovered Tumblr on her smartphone.
She dreamed of attending an elite college.
She was sometimes hostile at home.
She was very much loved.

She accepted an offer to an elite college.
She became an activist in multiple causes.
She was immersed in an alternative Tumblr world.
She wore a strapless black dress to prom.
She engaged in black and white thinking.
She was very much loved.

She wasn't present even when she was present.
She went off to college.
She seemed okay for a while.
She was not okay.
She wasn't sleeping much.
She was faraway, far away from home.
She was very much loved.

She arrived home for a visit.
She had a queer demeanour.
She was very thin.
She wore a wispy moustache, baggy clothes.
She was always on her phone—not present.
She was very much loved.

She left home suddenly.
She did not return.
"She is killing herself! She is killing all of us!"
(Said her mother collapsed on the floor.)
She went dark on social media.
She refused contact with her family.
She was very much loved.

She made a trans pronouncement from afar.
She was prescribed testosterone at her college's health centre.
She changed her name—first and last names.
She had her breasts excised.
She is barely recognisable to those who have known and loved her.
She was very much loved.
She is loved.

• • • •

Her mother

65

Genderfeels are a luxury

What happened with JKR shocked me and opened my eyes, the depth of the fury against her for statements which I fully agreed with and seemed very common sense was disproportionate. I'd always been very liberal, live and let live, fiercely supportive of free speech.

Because of what I saw, I decided to look into the matter more closely and found *r/gendercritical*. Reading the 'peak trans' threads was enlightening, because they were full of women like me, who didn't hate or wish harm on anyone but weren't willing to cede their existence

I watched the slow creep of, 'we just want to live as we are' to 'We're female and have periods too, bigots', as same-sex attraction was demonized and the progressives I knew suddenly sounded like the worst authoritarian homophobes and racists I had ever heard. Confusing!

For me, I hope everyone lives their best life. That does not include compelling the speech of others nor expecting obvious falsehoods to be upheld in an enforced *folie à plusieurs*. The truth matters. Objective reality and observable facts matter. Genderfeels are a luxury.

My ex has schizophrenia and it took me YEARS to feel confident in what was true and real after being caught in someone else's insanity. To then be told to disregard the evidence of my eyes and ears, to be seen as a second class citizen, I cannot abide.

So I fight.

· · · ·

Anandamide

66

Slow burn

For me, there wasn't a single moment where I suddenly peaked. Instead, it was a growing uncertainty about the narrative I was being fed. It was a scepticism, a questioning. I've never been one to get caught up in anything at all. Instead, I've always liked to take a step back and ask, "Why is this happening? Who is saying this? Why are they saying it? What are the alternative views? What evidence is there?"

My curiosity grew.

I came at this as a blank slate, but one who seeks the truth. The more I learned, the more I questioned, and the more I became sure that my feelings of unease were valid and wise. I had no reason to be sceptical. I grew up in a non-religious, non-political family, (we/I am slightly left of centre and politics was never a 'thing' for us).

As my concerns surrounding gender identity ideology grew, I learned my 50 year- old brother was to now transition to be a 'woman'. Out of the blue, after years of me joking that he was going through a mid-life crisis with his choice of car, leather jacket and becoming vegan after never caring about anything like that. After his wife left him and their child, and after a couple of girlfriends that didn't work out, he suddenly, out of the blue, announced he was becoming a woman.

This only confirmed my feelings. This isn't something inherently biological, this is physiological. This is about mental health, this is about trauma, even autism for many. This is about internalized homosexuality for some. And, for corporations and health care companies, as well as the media and politicians, it's about money, it's about votes. It's about power. And it's predominantly children who will suffer.

I only joined Twitter to fight this fight. I hate social media with a passion. But I hate gender ideology more. And I'm not talking about the people it affects.

I hate no-one.

But I hate the ideology and what its caused. Especially the harm to women and children.

• • • •

Concerned Mother of 3, Texas

67

For Fox sake

My origin story was Fallon Fox in 2012. I was a huge fan of MMA at the time, and thought it was absurd to allow a male to fight a female. There really isn't any sport where the consequences are more devastating than in MMA.

It pissed me the fuck off that some people were pretending that this was in any way OK, or fair. I thought the absurdity of it all would stop it in its track right then and there. Boy, was I wrong... I've been vocal about my GC views ever since.

After the Fallon Fox incident, I kept paying attention to the other avenues where 'Gender Identity' was wreaking havoc, especially when it came to youth and children. Young people who displayed unconventional interests and hobbies were guided into an ideology that encouraged them to 'transition'. I thought back to my own childhood. I played football (soccer), hated wearing dresses because it wasn't practical, my father gave me tools so I could help him out with construction on our house from the time I could walk (I was probably not very helpful at the time). I had no interest in conventional girl things. I feared that if someone like me were to grow up in today's climate, she would be pushed towards transition. Never once during my childhood/youth did I ever think I was anything but a girl, because no one put such ideas in my head.

I grew up and turned out to be a lesbian, with my body and mind intact. I was allowed to figure things out in my own time, on my own terms. Gender non-conforming kids today won't be so lucky. I will fight this madness every step of the way.

This is the hill I will die on.

. . . .

Siri J. Bodin (Norway)

68

A bubble of woke

I started from a very much woke but ignorant side. Essentially I believed that people could be born in the wrong body and that trans women were women. I even had an argument with my dad trying to lecture him that 4-year-olds who really believed they were the opposite sex, must be.

I was appalled when a person at work transitioned and the email still had his dead name for a few weeks and told colleagues how appalling that was.

I was in a very woke bubble on Twitter so when people were talking about Graham Linehan and how he 'just wouldn't leave trans people alone', I just assumed that he was just spewing hate and wondered why Twitter hadn't banned him already. Of course, I never saw the opposite argument and therefore assumed transwomen were people that had had the 'full operation'.

I was so ignorant that when I saw people on Mumsnet moaning about Mermaids I thought they were talking about people who believed they were literally mermaids!

Then one day I was watching velodrome cycling on the BBC Red button and saw a male cyclist racing in the women's category and I knew that was wrong. I tried to justify it in my head by thinking, "Oh well, at least it isn't the Olympics" or, "Well those are the official rules" - but since that didn't help I decided to just not think about it and take the fingers in the ears approach.

Slowly though, I began to read some of those threads on Twitter that I had been ignoring. One person commented that *transwomen were based on female stereotypes* and I couldn't get that would of my head - after all, I considered myself a feminist. Eventually I found myself lurking on the mumsnet feminist boards and my Twitter feed began to look more and more *terfy* and I began to disagree with my *woke Twitter bubble*.

Then, of course, I sat down and read J. K. Rowling's essay (I'd been ignoring that for a few months) and everything in there articulated how I was feeling.

Since then it's been a very steep learning curve! So it's been a very long process and I wish I had been one of those people who never bought into it in the first place - but I got there eventually.

. . . .

Anon

69

When the dysphoria fades

My origin story starts around 2014 when I first discovered gender identity. Prior to this I, like most people rarely thought about trans people, and my understanding was that *trans* was someone (usually a male) who was very feminine and fully, medically transitioned.

They were very much an extreme minority who I viewed sympathetically. I had never heard of a trans man before this. The context of me finding gender ideology is someone with depression and anxiety. I had experienced some trauma in my childhood and had homophobic family members. I was someone who was insecure and unhappy with myself, and very much disliked the way I was sometimes treated and viewed in our society for being female. I remember seeing a television drama about a trans man, something I had never even considered before, and the story resonated with me. It planted a seed that I kept thinking about, and like most people when they want to understand something, I looked online. I searched for 'How do you know if you are trans?', and I found myself on forums and support groups, and the answer they gave sent me down the rabbit hole. "If you think you might be trans, you probably are. Cis people never question their gender."

This led me to YouTube, and I was presented with story after story of miserable, odd-looking women who were transformed into smiling, good looking men. The videos all followed a similar structure, timelines and voice comparisons and gushing joy about how they were now happy, free and successful. Top surgery videos were common and taking 'T' was talked about like it was as simple as taking a vitamin pill. Indeed, one *trans influencer* even described it like that.

Nothing about the health risks of surgery or hormones was ever mentioned that I can remember. The narrative was only one of progressive happiness. What made it harder to resist was all the 'respectable' and official web pages that backed up the narrative. Organisations I assumed were legitimate and an authority like

Stonewall described gender as something innate to all of us, and how no surgery or anything else was required: it was all about you and your personal journey. What was undeniable was the clear idea that so-called 'cis people' were those who conformed and were comfortable doing so, and those of us who weren't were trans and non-binary. I certainly didn't 'identify' with being a woman or femininity, indeed the idea made me very uncomfortable, and now I had my answer. All my unhappiness and not fitting in throughout my life was because I was trying to live a lie as the wrong gender. Non binary soon turned to trans man, and the ideas and rhetoric I saw filled my head. Just some of the things I thought at the time include that there was no real difference between males and females so prisons etc., shouldn't be an issue, gender expression is beautiful and freeing, tom boys from the past were probably trans, and transition is a journey of self-discovery. I even came out to a couple of people as trans, who were very supportive, and I joined local trans social groups.

However, even I could see the cognitive dissonance, even then. I knew deep down my views about women had become very sexist. I thought I wasn't a woman because I didn't identify with that role and didn't have that personality and mindset. But of course, that can only logically mean that I believed woman are the people in society who do have a certain mindset and behaviour. One based entirely on sexist stereotypes because there is no other possible way of defining it without biology. This, as a feminist, was something I had always rejected, and knew it was regressive, but I rationalised it by referring to the official websites on the topic who all backed it up, and by me experiencing dysphoria about my body and wanting to look male.

Fast forward a few years and I was utterly obsessed with my gender and transitioning and decided to have weekly counselling. However, by my second counsellor I found the more I put the work in long term to address other issues and trauma, the more the feeling of dysphoria and discomfort with my sex eased. I was also doing my own research on the health implications, being a bit of a hypochondriac. I had accepted what may happen by taking testosterone, such as hair loss and potential cancer risk in the future, but as I looked further, I discovered the issues of atrophy and the need long term for a hysterectomy. This information was very hard to find, and there was nothing on the trans sites about the consequences of the operation and a potential early menopause if the ovaries were also removed, so I looked on pages for women who'd had the procedure. It was here I discovered it is major surgery that could have a huge impact on sexual function and could even increase the risk of dementia.

I felt very uncomfortable that none of this was ever discussed by trans influencers, and I was not blind to the clear issues with mental illness in other people in a similar situation, both online and in person, and the undeniable reliance on sexist stereotypes threaded throughout the narrative.. I had started to realise how easy and quickly it had sucked me in when I was at a low point and made me obsess for years, and how little sense the actual arguments made when objectively scrutinised. It was all slogans and with no answers. What does feeling like a woman actually mean? What is non binary without stereotypes? Neuroscience said there is no such thing as a man's brain, so how can one think like a man?

It became harder to reconcile the inconsistencies. I was told *sex is spectrum* and trans people don't need to want to undergo any sort of medical transition, or even have dysphoria to be trans, but on the other hand trans children needed urgent access to blockers to prevent secondary sex characteristics and cross sex hormones were called lifesaving treatment. Conversely, it was just as strongly asserted there's no such thing as a man or woman's body, and a woman can have a penis and even a thick beard and be a 'lesbian with a beard' - as an activist associated with Stonewall asserted. This was the first time it occurred it to me that it was like a cult.

It was at this time, when the dysphoria like feeling about my body had faded, and I was jaded about the movement that I created an anonymous account on Facebook in order to discuss political issues freely.

It was here that I started reading feminist arguments and seeing discussions that chimed with what I had always previously believed to be true, that gender was a regressive social construct, and men and women can have any personality, and dress and behave in any way they like, that androgyny should be celebrated not medicalised and pathologised. I also become aware for the first time how women were being erased in language and referred to by terms like cervix havers in a way that wasn't happening to men. I started watching videos from groups like a woman's place and saw the clash of Posie Parker and Adrian Harrop. I was able to see potential issues with a clear head. Sex offenders in female prisons, sports, women's changing rooms and toilets being made unisex - one even with a urinal left in. This was around 2018 and was the first time I started calling myself *gender critical*, which just meant to me that I was critical of gender as the feminine and masculine stereotypes. I didn't really think of it as being about trans issues at that time. However, while the feminist arguments I was reading and joining in with were logical and made sense, it was TRAs themselves, and their behaviour that had a huge impact on my mindset. I was still very supportive and sympathetic of trans people and saw myself as just critical of some of the ideas, and the impact they could have, especially on younger people. I thought I could have sensible and respectful, fact-based discussions with trans activists.

I have never been more wrong.

I was shocked to discover there was no middle ground and no compromise whatsoever. I had to agree sex doesn't matter at all in any circumstance or I was a hateful bigoted TERF and there was nothing I could say, no experience or evidence I could give and no point clearly expressed that would persuade them otherwise. In addition, the accounts were the most aggressive and sexist people I have ever come across in my life. Violent threats about bricking women in the face were in the replies to Pink News articles, images with guns and baseball bats were sent, and there were posts about them finding people's addresses and getting them fired. It was horrifying and hasn't let up since then, the latest being men in balaclavas yelling at women.

There were two things that finally pushed me over the edge to a full rejection of gender ideology. The first was seeing a safe sex guide aimed at teenagers from Scotland. It was for lesbians and contained many pages about how to have sex and pleasure with someone with a penis. I was shocked and found the gay men's guide from the same company. It had no information about a vagina, and neither did the straight women's guide. I found the one for straight men and could hardly believe it to see like the others there was nothing about pleasuring a penis. It was only the lesbian guide, aimed at teenagers. It was deliberate, homophobic, and sexist beyond doubt.

The second was on a left-wing political page where I was

discussing Female Genital Mutilation (FGM), something that turns my stomach with how evil and barbaric it is. I got a warning for using 'gendered language'.

I couldn't understand what was happening. Surely they could see the entire drive of FGM is an attack on the body of women, of million of girls all over the world. If you erased sex - you erased the horrific sexism. To try and claim FGM isn't about women is so insulting to all the survivors.

For this opinion I was banned from the group and have since seen actual FGM survivors attacked by TRAs for the same reason.

I had peaked.

. . .

CJ

70

No thank you

In the year 2015 I was browsing through Twitter. My feed at the time was full of nerd stuff and I was interested in the arts. One of my music *Tweeps* posted a link to an article on, 'Daphne Shaed, Hindu tranny cyborg. A woman with a penis'.

The article complained about Shaed being made Women's Services Coordinator at a university in Australia, on the basis of his wang showing through the ladies undies he was posing in. Bear in mind that this was the age of Hayley Cropper from Coronation Street - a transgender character played by a woman on a British soap opera. Hayley was portrayed as harmless, lovable, and vulnerable. While I didn't watch the show, I was aware of the character and felt sorry for her. I wanted her to be happy. I had also read many articles on transsexuals (as they were called) and had come to the conclusion that transsexuals were like Harmless Hayley - misunderstood and in need of compassion. I also believed that their distress drove them to have a complete bodily surgical transformation to resemble a woman so closely they were a human version of *I can't believe it's not butter* - that you'd have to look hard to tell the difference. Of course this meant that my reaction to Shaed was that he couldn't possibly be the real thing since he didn't want bottom surgery and not only was he not ashamed or upset about having a penis he couldn't help talking about having one - and showing it off. *Hang on,* I thought, *if he's not the real thing, why is he a) demanding to be treated as a woman at all times and in all ways, and b) why in the world is anyone going along with it?*

I found myself agreeing with some rather harsh-sounding women that he was indeed a fetishist and that he shouldn't be in women-only spaces. I could not accept that he was anything but an anomaly. I wrote a blog post about how difficult it must be to live with dysphoria only to have it mocked by the likes of Shaed, and concluded that we ought to be wary of Shaeds but be kind to the Harmless Hayleys. And not to be too quick to pass judgement.

Then I learned that Shaed had hollowed out Women's Services at the University and repurposed it as a 'gender identity club'. When people stopped using it, the service shut down.

I wasn't really paying attention to this issue but was aware that straight men like Alex Drummond were describing themselves as lesbians and that the people who should have been protesting this were being written off as bigots. I started asking questions to find out more and befriended those transsexuals who were willing to answer them. This continued until J. K. Rowling wrote that *Dress how you please* tweet. When I saw the abuse she was getting for it I got off the fence and sided with her on the grounds that people who have a point, make the point. They don't need to resort to abuse or make wild accusations.

I wrote many blog posts trying to make sense of what was going on, trying to maintain a middle ground position. I saw reasonable trans folk derided as 'truscum' and quislings - because they wouldn't join in with the abuse and because they were reasonable and not given to hysterical rhetoric.

I started to question what Rowling was saying because of all the nasty comments by looking up the issues she was raising. Every point was proven to be true.

I saw Dr. Sidbh Gallagher's TikTok 'Yeet the teets' videos back up Rowling's assertions about kids having double mastectomies, academics suing universities for shutting down research into detransitioners, the Keira Bell lawsuit, the destruction of women's careers for liking *the wrong tweets* and, in one case, for asking a question on Mumsnet. The final straw came in 2019 when I was researching a blog post on astroturfing RE: trans issues and I asked a free speech advocate about it. His response was to basically call me a hateful bigot and his mates joined in. People I had known for years suddenly decided that I was a Nazi. They'd had four years to direct-message me to discuss the matter but preferred to announce that they thought the worst of me in public. I abandoned them and threw my lot in with the TERFs.

I was still using preferred pronouns, etc., but had decided that there were two types of 'T': fetishist perverts taking advantage of public sympathy to exploit and abuse women, and the nice dysphoric ones that were mostly harmless. My sympathies remain with the second group. I continued to ask questions and was persuaded by the calm, rational, reasonable people who answered me. I carried out Zoom interviews with a male-to-female transitioner (MTF) and the mother of a trans teen. I even bought dinner for an 'MTF' as I struggled to understand what was happening. My patience with the pronouns thing snapped when Laurel Hubbard was admitted to the New Zealand weightlifting team instead of Roviel Detenamo: a white millionaire's son took the place of an indigenous woman on the grounds of adopting a woman's name, growing his hair long, and using 'she/her'.

I will never forget the interview with the women afterwards. The dignified, "No thank you", said a great deal more than those three words can convey.

#WiSpa followed, then #Chris Chan. That was it; no more pronouns. I'll use an asterisk to escape a ban if I must. I keep getting re-peaked by the ridiculous behaviour of trans rights activists and the absurdities of gender identity ideology.

It's an authoritarian quasi-religious cult.

• • •

Wendy, Manchester

71

Brighton sock

An 'origin story'. Thing is, I don't actually have one. I've had friends, some of them close friends, that identify as transgender for over 25 years and at no point in all those years did they, I, or anybody else we know not have a clear grasp of reality. When the GRA 2004 came in I felt a flicker of, "Well, that's a bit mad", but nobody I know has applied for one because that would be daft; we all know what's what.

I think **the** *moment* for me was looking at 2015 and comparing it to 2002. In 2002 Fatboy Slim played Brighton beach (I live in Brighton) and quite apart from the litter, one of the things that happened was a *lot* of people that knew less than shit about how Brighton works came to town. I was not at the gig and just went to the pub, and was walking home with a lesbian friend of mine and a male friend who identifies as transgender. Suddenly this small group of yobs come from nowhere, screaming about fucking queers. It was my male friend that they decide to beat up. He ended up with a broken jaw. (This was very lucky, because walking to the hospital was an option; there is no way an ambulance could have got through, a) the crowds and, b) the litter, had it been a broken leg).

So we are in hospital. My friend with the broken jaw, 'S', is treated with the utmost courtesy at all times. But is treated realistically. S was going to be kept in overnight (not least because the hospital was under a lot of pressure that night) and - while there was clearly no question of being simply bunged into a men's ward, there was equally no question of a women's ward; this was discussed at calm, caring and intelligent length (not in those terms) with S, and with me and my other friend who were still with her. It was decided (not least because of the extreme circumstances of the Fatboy Slim gig) that S would stay in the A&E section overnight and that we would, unusually, be allowed to stay too. This worked for everybody.

Fast forward to 2015 and thousands of people are signing a petition to have a man convicted of a very violent crime (and with a history of it) put in a women's prison just because he's had some cosmetic surgery / taken some drugs (Tara Hudson).

At this point I realised that 'the system' had stopped trying to work to help individual people, and was instead going to force my friend S (next time there was a broken jaw incident, though thankfully that has not happened) to make women in hospital feel uncomfortable.

And at that point I thought 'all this 'policy' and 'best practice' crap is being put out by people that know less than nothing about it.

• • •

Anon

72

Peaked, working for the NSPCC

I sort of knew something was going on but I had no idea what and I didn't really want to know either as it seemed so toxic. I was in crisis due to having gone to the police about historical child sex abuse in 2015 and I couldn't cope with more trauma.

Even so, and as part of my personal healing process, I decided to join *Childline* after seeing a film called *Sulphur and White* which really moved me. I joined in 2020 and started to hear more about 'trans' but still didn't really know what was going on. It seemed like such a big row, and I had to stay away from it for my own sanity.

The first red flag was in training, before I even started. The trainer, a man, exhibited MRA (Men's RIghts Activist) beliefs right off the bat, which I knew about very well as my brother had become a woman-hating MRA after getting addicted to coke and Alex Jones - in that order - in the noughties, after which the only two words he managed to say to me began with F and B - in that order. The trainer talked about boys being in as much risk, if not more, for sexual assault as girls, and when queried on the stats we all know very well he said, boys don't report. As a girl who had not reported when I was a child, I felt sick to my stomach at this blatant lie.

Even so *Childline* has been an amazing experience and it is a great privilege to be able to help children. I reply to emails from kids who need help or just want someone to talk to. Nine out of ten of the young people contacting *Childline* are girls. Recently there was a push to get boys to use the service, and they had tried to include 'trans' boys in there but I guess they decided that was bad idea as I noticed, whenever I could bear to look, that this had dropped out of their marketing. And nine out of the ten young people I helped during that time and after continued to be girls.

I had a couple of emails with trans themes early on. It was

clear to me these children were extremely distraught, totally confused about what they were, and suffering. I answered them in a common sense way, pointing out that labels are not important and can frequently change, and what's important is what's inside. I guess that wasn't protocol but I wasn't aware of it.

Then I had an email from a 13-year-old girl who had been *binding* and had been using a boy's name, but this particular email was to let us know that after chatting with her parents she had changed her mind and was a girl again.

I had heard about the mastectomies around that time and was getting concerned. The very same day, we had been instructed to be very conscious not to deadname or mis-pronoun kids who had requested these things, and it was obvious that someone senior had done a search through all the accounts and written in red capitals on all confused gender accounts to USE CORRECT PRONOUNS AND NOT TO DEADNAME, and this young girl's account had all this all over it, and here I was saying, "That's great, it sounds like your parents really care about you", "You did the right thing", etc.

When it came for a supervisor to check over my response, she was most insistent that I use the boy's name that the girl had been using previously, I guess keen to follow these BIG RED CAPITAL LETTERS on the account details.

We had a very robust discussion and I told her I was not willing to do that as the girl had changed her mind and I did not want to be influencing the child. The supervisor was most insistent I did, but I didn't back down, and in the end we compromised and I asked the girl to confirm what she wanted to be called going forward.

My ears were really pricking up.

More conscious of the red flags, I started to see more examples of extreme dodginess. For example, an 11-year-old girl, totally confused about gender, suggesting having adult friends in chat rooms, and being told by supervisors not to explore that.

Noticing other volunteers asking for a distraught child's preferred pronouns before saying anything else at all to them.

Reading email responses to gender-confused kids from *Childline* volunteers telling them that J.K. Rowling is a bad person for her views.

And on and on.

And I would not be surprised if there was a list of gender-friendly volunteers who respond to the gender-confused kids as I don't get assigned these emails anymore.

Childline themselves agree with the ACE questionnaire knowledge and neuroscience generally that children's brains, up to when they're in their mid-20s, are in development and thus vulnerable and very malleable, which they take pains to detail in their online training, so why they have been actively ignoring that and pushing autistic and troubled (mostly) girls towards sterilisation, mutilation, and drugs for the rest of their lives is totally beyond me.

I eventually heard about the bizarre AGP behaviour that went on at *Childline* before my time, and was truly horrified, and I guess they have been infiltrated in unimaginable ways by unimaginable people, as you might expect a children's charity would be.
There is a sense of not being able to speak about the child abuse going on before our very eyes, while other volunteers just seem to be completely in the dark about it, and of course many are also fully TRA.

What I would like to say is that *Childline* is for the most part an amazing service to children. The way this trans thing has taken hold of normal people's rational minds and turned them into paedophile-apologisers and worse, if there could be worse, is truly astonishing.

Childline and other children's charities are going to have to do the right thing, apologise, weed out the rot, and change, and the sooner the better.

• • •

Anon

73

The long good 'why'

Eight years ago I came across this study. At the time I was a young woman entering STEM education (since switched to humanities). Prior to this, I naively believed same work = same pay.

Health and family circumstances forged a different path for me. I switched to art. When the National Gallery made a big song and dance about collecting *A. Gentileschi*, I learned they only had a handful of female artists in their collection.

Of course, female artists and collectives have been highlighting the disparity for decades. The one thing that was clear to me in every industry was an overt signalling of sex automatically meant less pay, fewer opportunities, more open to prejudice. So my CVs became initialled.

But then came the pronouns. Suddenly that 'S' initial held no protection from sex discrimination. I was now expected to declare, with enthusiasm, my sex. At introductions, to dutifully repeat the mantra she/her she/her, no matter how pointless it was when *third person* was never used.

This moment was my catalyst to become more involved. I'd never heard of *peak trans* until the start of this year. I still don't know if I'm even there yet. Every few days I reach greater peaks, it seems to come in waves of disbelief.

So why now? Why bother wading into this shit?

Because it matters. I've sat back and seen enough from people who I thought I was aligned with. Peddling out slogans, chants, mantras with zero substance or grounding in reality. It came as a shock when I realised they meant what they said in the most literal sense.

They meant trans people really were the opposite sex. They meant prostitution really was a viable, nay, desirable career choice. This wasn't about breaking down stigma and offering help to individuals, this was a 're-education'. They really, truly, believe in more than two sexes.

This was demonstrated by one of the world's most famous authors (not that one), tweeting that sex was a 'bell curve' and referencing *Scientific American*. I couldn't believe my eyes, particularly as her novels are so heavily referenced in this 'debate', second only to *1984*.

And now we have the issue of Self ID. I sat with tears watching a man sit before the Scottish Government's panel saying, "There's no conflict with self ID and women's safety, privacy or rights." The women sitting behind him shook their heads, bit their tongues.

For me, it epitomised this entire shit show. Women have lost their careers and livelihoods. Academics have been hunted out of institutions. Students have been investigated for saying women have vaginas. Artists have been ousted from their industry. In short, it's a witch hunt.

This all happens against the noisy background of intimidation, physical assault, rape threats, death threats, racism and anti-semitism. Anyone who dares speak out is treated like a pariah. No one is exempt, from school children to pensioners.

Very clearly women are saying, *"NO."*

I used to think no one was listening, now it's blatantly obvious they are listening but just don't care. Ignorance I can forgive, arrogance I cannot. Seeing the concerted effort to stigmatise and disassociate from anyone who thinks sex is real and gender is not.

To cast them as alt-right religious fundamentalists, hell-bent on the eradication (?) of anyone 'under the rainbow'. Projecting this false narrative seeks to create an *us versus them* binary. This is reinforced with the 'right side of history' mantra.

Members of what can only be described at this stage as a cult, receive all their information through a filter. Just the other day a friend shared an info graphic with disinformation which listed *GenderGP* as one of the sources - this was after Mike Webberley had been struck off.

Realising I was getting truth from The Daily Mail, The Telegraph and The Times was a huge wake-up call. The Guardian wasn't touching any of this with a barge pole, the BBC was rewriting witness statements and apologising for reporting the findings of their own investigations.

The thing that finally made me sign up to Twitter - which I swore I never would - was simply networking. We all have our own story, how we got here, how much we know, how disillusioned we feel.

I think it's imperative women meet, organise and discuss the threats to our existence.

. . .

S

Another side of things

It was early 2018, I lived in LA, and I was posting on Facebook in support of trans bathroom bills in NC when I got a Direct Message from a friend I hadn't seen in about five years. She was a lesbian, a mom - a kind of crunchy granola. She said, "I just wanted you to know that the issue isn't as simple as you think... I just wanted to know if you're open to hearing the other side."
 I said, "Yes, sure", because, to be honest, Caitlyn Jenner winning *Woman of the Year* did bother me, I had some nagging questions, but also had a belief that things would work out okay.

 And I really hate the phrase 'rights aren't pie'. I could never square that with the history of women fighting for their rights.
 Anyway, I said, "Yes, I'm open to hearing another side." And she said, "Here's a link to the *Cotton Ceiling*." And then, "Here's Magdalen Berns' YouTube videos."

 Lastly she said, "I'm deleting this thread. We can never ever talk about this again, but I just wanted you to know."

 But I watched those videos and followed the link and now I'm really trying to help as much as I can. She and I have never spoken about it again. I'm sure we've crossed paths on Twitter, but I have no idea.

 She was my GC-lesbian-guardian angel.

• • • •

MJ Austen

75

It's a big hill to die on

I am a school leader and have been a head and deputy head-teacher across a variety of contexts, so I have a vast experience of over 20 years of education, plus 46 years as a human female. I am gender non-conforming, as is my autistic pre-teen daughter.

I fell into motherhood with my son 15 years ago and stumbled across Mumsnet, without which I would probably have just cried. I explored Mumsnet avidly over the years and, approximately eight years ago, I learned about AGP (autogynephilia) and joined Twitter.

Well, there you have it, my story.

I am out to others as *Gender Critical* and have battled to keep the toxic ideology from being taught in my school and challenged it at my children's schools and where I am a governor. I have been challenged, but I stayed strong. It's the bloody big hill I thought I will either die on or lose my job over.

Although maybe less so now!

. . . .

Anon

76

Birth of a TERF!

A friend of mine went to the *Anarchist Bookfair* in October 2017 and witnessed the hounding of Helen Steel at that event. At the bookfair a mob of activists had gathered around Helen and were shouting abuse at her and ordering her to leave the bookfair. The reported basis for the attack was that Helen was a transphobe and TERF because she had supported the right of women to hand out leaflets that were critical of the government's proposal to make changes to the Gender Recognition Act.

My friend was very shaken up by what he had witnessed and in particular the mob-like nature of the attack on a woman and fellow activist. At the time, I was a 'be kind' left-leaning liberal and I would have considered myself to be a trans ally (although I never believed that 'trans women are women', not understanding that this already put me firmly in TERF territory).

The idea that Helen Steel was a bigot and a transphobe just didn't add up for me. I had always admired her as an activist and a campaigner and I just couldn't believe that this was correct.

In the aftermath of the bookfair, I spent the next few months down a rabbit hole (on Mumsnet, YouTube and Twitter) trying to find out as much information as possible watching and following people on both sides of the debate and trying to work out what I thought from a properly informed perspective.

My 'be kind' position quickly crumbled in the face of an ideology that I discovered was post-truth, anti-science and authoritarian. It probably helped that I already believed in the immutability of biological sex so really all I had to do was come to terms with the idea that I was now considered to be on the 'wrong-side of history'.

I also hadn't previously realised that trans activism was already pushing for trans women to be able to compete in women's sports and be placed in women's prisons and that puberty blocking drugs were not evidence-based treatment so my previous position had been from a place of ignorance.

• • • •

Anon

77

A can of worms

My origin story has two parts. The first was when a local trans-identified male made national news because they had been sent to a male prison. I was outraged. I have never believed anyone could change sex but I felt it was kinder to see them the way they wanted us to.

I saw a transwoman in an awful wig and badly fitting outfit at a *Job Centre* back in the 80s and I remember how their hands trembled. They seemed to me as sensitive as an exposed nerve. My heart went out to them, and I made up a whole story in my head about how vulnerable and tragic they were.

So when I learned of the person being sent to a male prison, my mind immediately went back to that day in the *Job Centre*. Once I added that memory to my own personal knowledge of how some men can be bigots and bullies, and what I thought I knew about how violent prisons are, I feared for this person's safety.

But then I read a local Facebook thread discussing this person. People I knew said this person was a violent and dangerous criminal too. Learning this information made me question if they were really the victim they were being portrayed as in the media.

The second part of my story involved the lovely *Glinner*. Somehow, I stumbled across a thread on Twitter where wave after wave of people were attacking him for an episode of The IT Crowd that featured a trans-identified male (TIM).

I was stunned to read people calling him a bigot and a transphobe, so I felt I should speak up. I commented that the TIM was in no way a victim in that storyline. The fight scene - which I found hysterical - showed 'her' kicking Reynholm's arse. The storyline ended with Reynholm pining for his lost love. So I spoke up in defence of Graham. Boy, did I ever open a can of worms. I was told that it was 'hateful' for him to show a transwoman displaying male aggression and that Graham was a well known bigot. At first, I apologised - I was totally new to this issue and assumed there was something I was missing, and that I should listen to those who felt discriminated against. As a woman of colour, I empathised with anyone whose grievances were being ignored. But in my gut, I just couldn't agree with what they were saying.

I learned Glinner is basically a decent man who is trying to do the right thing and I saw how everything he said and did was being twisted and intentionally misunderstood. That's when I realised - something was very, very wrong with the current discourse about this issue, and that women - particularly lesbians - were being silenced and bullied.

I thought back to the transwoman who I'd signed a petition for to help get them get sent to a women's prison, and I was ashamed.

. . . .

MsChopsy

78

Friends, lost and found

I had no idea about any of it, until one day my 13-year-old autistic daughter came downstairs saying she thought she was a boy. It came completely out of left field. I had studied psychology at university and was aware of gender dysphoria in very young children, especially boys. But not this. So I started researching online and I came across a whole swathe of stuff relating to it. I had to parse the nonsense from the true. I found Lisa Littman and Abigail Shriers' book. Read it in one sitting. Took about one to two weeks to sweat over what to do, until I decided to ban the internet and phone from my girl.

She had been watching a lot of YouTube tutorials of trans people doing make up, etc. She loved one who has now been found to be a predator. She already hated her body and felt so out of touch with other girls because of her autism. She tried to run away from home, but we live in middle of nowhere so it only lasted a day!

Around six months later she seemed to wake up, and recently (she's 17 now) expressed feeling like she was falling down a black hole, and that she was grateful that I took drastic measures. She is now trying to come to terms with the hatred she feels for her body by working out, etc., but she is very happy being female. She was also questioning her sexuality at the time, which added a lot of confusion to her too.

Since then I have been very vocal on Facebook under my real name, which has made me lose friends, but also gain new ones.

• • • •

Anon

79

The shifting Sands

My true peaking moment (I'd had a few before but this one solidified my resolve) was when *Sands*, a charity for bereaved parents who have lost a baby to stillbirth, miscarriage and neonatal death, posted about 'birthing parents' - meaning *Mothers*.

Many of us who have lost a baby and who have accessed *Sands* for support explained that the word 'Mother' is extremely important to us. Freddy McConnell and cronies said we were all 'weaponising our trauma' against the 'trans community'.

After that I asked why not both 'Mother/mums and birthing parents' if inclusion was really the intention. I received many mocking replies and some anon accounts even trolled me about my baby lost to stillbirth.

Then I learned first-hand the hatred many of the 'activists' behind the 'transwomen are women' slogan have for non-believers.

I no longer sought to compromise on language, or anything when it comes to the honest truth again after that.

. . . .

Kelly W

80

The mess we're in

I was aware trans was becoming a thing, Caitlyn Jenner had come out, India Willoughby had shown the true face of transactivism on Celebrity Big Brother and our babysitter was a transman. But it wasn't until the lesbians demonstrated at *Pride* in London in the summer of 2018 that I truly peaked.

Their brave demo came up on my Facebook feed. I read the story and thought, "Yeah, lesbians don't have penises." So I shared the story with the comment, "I think they have a point."

I was instantly set upon by people I had once considered friends - mostly males, mostly bearded. But there were some women too. Those who were adamant 'sex work is work'. I was called a 'bigot' and a 'TERF' and that I should 'educate myself'. And then fatalistically someone mentioned Glinner.

I had started using twitter in 2016 but had never heard of Glinner! I searched his name and promptly fell down the rabbit hole. I bumped into some of the big name transactivists on the way down, spending a whole night arguing with three I won't name. But the next day I felt horrified, gaslit and a bit in shock. I soon found MKRH and Jane Clare Jones and before I knew it I was fully educated and a full-on TERF.

• • • •

Jen

81

Here's the thing: I am scared

See, I joined twitter a few months ago in a different ID, to discuss Labour politics. I like lefty Twitter. I'm happy there. I'm a party member.

I knew nothing about the GRA debate at that point; but did see mentions of transphobia. Naturally, I was against that. I saw as well mention of horrible bigoted people called 'TERFs' and obviously I was against them too. And when I learnt what 'TERF' stands for, I was surprised: *What's happened to feminism over the last 20 years or so while I haven't been paying attention? Has it got nasty?* I thought, *I'll investigate further.*

Start with Stonewall; they're a respectable authority.

They say, "Trans women are women."

I am a woman. And a feminist, albeit one who's a bit out of practice. And this doesn't immediately compute, because, well, what makes me a woman?
Two things: (1) biology; (2) the intense socialisation-from-birth process that goes into the creation of a female.

Which of those does a transwoman share? Neither. So I can't at first glance see any mechanism by which they could be a woman. "Trans women are women," doesn't make sense to me.

I'm not against it, you understand. I just don't see it.

But I may be wrong not to. I may be out of date. After all, my grandma sincerely believed that having children out of wedlock was wrong. That belief made sense to her; but it's one that hasn't stood the test of time. Maybe my lack of comprehension about this will look ridiculous to my grandchildren. Maybe it will be obvious to them that trans women are women.

I need to look into this with an open mind. *WHY* are trans women, women? How? What is the reasoning behind that assertion?

I looked online for articles, videos, etc. First lesson: there's a lot out there saying TWAW, but surprisingly little saying WHY that's so. One article told me not to conflate biological sex with genitals, as though doing that was ridiculous. But it's no good, call me *grandma* if you will, but I DO conflate them. I'd need a bloody good argument to persuade me to change that view. I don't find one in the article. Another one says it's all about hormones *in utero*. Lots of female hormones cause a female brain to develop, occasionally in a male body. And it's the brain that determines your sex, not the body.

And this, apparently, is now understood by science, although I confess its discovery had passed me by.

The only problem with this (and admittedly I speak as a non-scientist) is that it's drivel. My mind may be open. But it isn't completely empty. (It's also those hormones, apparently, that result in the 'motivation to be visually attractive' in the female of the species. Which... oh, really, fuck it, life's too short). My open mind is wanting to creak shut at this point, but I tell it *no, absolutely not*, and I prop it open with cocktail sticks because I'm gonna keep looking.

Who knows what we'll find next?

What I found next was this: *Trans women are women AND THIS IS NOT UP FOR DEBATE.*

Ah! Bit of a brick wall there, comrades. I'm genuinely trying to understand your point of view. I'm considering adopting it as my own once I've understood it (after all, I don't want to be one of these horrible 'TERFs'). But help me out here! How can I if you won't discuss it?

Only it turns out that merely asking the question makes me a bigot. I know this because a man in a dress on YouTube tells me so, with maximum hostility. And I start to wonder: is it possible that the trans side of the debate has set the bar for bigotry just a bit too low?

So I read on. And I find a now infamous photograph of what appeared to be a trans woman wearing a t-shirt with "I punch TERFS" on it and covered in what looked like blood stains.

And I'll be honest, at this point it becomes too much for the cocktail sticks. They buckle and snap, and my mind begins to close. Because there is only so much I can be impartial about. And no, I don't know much about trans issues. But I know misogyny when I see it.

And yes, it bothers me. And it frightens me. Yes, I lose my objectivity at this point - and with it, the ability to keep my mind open. Which is just as well, because what I learn next would - if my mind was still open - have made my brain fall out.

- *Lesbians pressured to have sex with TW with penises? (How rapey is that?)*

- *TW in women's sport? How can this possibly be okay? Whoever thought it was?*

- *TW saying they're the only true representatives of womanhood (for reasons so ridiculous I can't be arsed to repeat them here)?*

And most of all, most tragically and awfully of all,

- *confused children being permanently deprived of their fertility and sexual function before they're old enough to choose their A-level subjects??*

And by this point I'm realising that maybe those awful TERFs might just possibly not be so awful after all. Maybe they've actually got a point. In fact, astonishingly, many of them seem hugely intelligent and insightful... and anything but bigoted. I'd like to discuss this in Labour circles. But here's the thing: I am scared.
I am ACTUALLY SCARED to put into words that I'm worried, that I think there are genuine issues to be considered, that there may be competing rights here.
Now, my cowardice is my own problem, and I can't blame anyone else for it. I know this. But for what it's worth, I'm a barrister: I argue, confront and piss people off for a living. I enjoy debate.

I don't think I've ever before found myself too scared to express my point of view before, ever, about anything. So, I do ask, "What is going on here?"

Yes, I'm pathetic. Yes, I ought to speak up and accept the ostracism that I know will follow. But I can't, at least not yet.

And much as that speaks volumes about me as an individual, I wonder - does it say something too about the debate itself?

Massive respect to those of you who have spoken up and taken the consequences.

Thank you for listening

. . . .

Anon

82

Nope!

I peaked after I objected to being called 'cis', this trans person was insisting that there was nothing wrong with being rebranded because I was being inclusive.

I was having none of that.

I began to look further into this trans issue, and I came across the Magdalen Berns video of *Alex* who claimed he was a lesbian and that was it for me, further digging then led me to Self-ID.

Nope. I was having none of that.

I wasn't going to allow any man to just claim to be a woman, I felt insulted by that, but worse was to come, the detransitioner stories started to appear, and then they came for the children.

Again, I was having none of that either!

• • • •

Sandra Taylor,
Mother, Grandmother,
Registered Veterinary Nurse

Common sense will prevail

I must have been in my teens when I saw a programme about a transsexual woman who was fighting to get their birth documents changed to show female rather than male. The programme was very sympathetic and like most watchers, I guess, I thought, "What's the harm? - of course he should be able to say he's a 'woman'."

In the intervening years I can't say I thought much about it. Then I saw an interview with Germaine Greer - by then I had two daughters of my own. I always liked Germaine but didn't always agree with her. But as I loved the whole Peter Cook, Private Eye feel of the 60s, Germaine was always worth listening to.

In the interview she said something which I thought was quite obvious, *men are not women.* What piqued my interest was why she was so vehement about it. So I started looking on the internet and found Magdalen Berns and Jenni Murray on Radio 4. I realised that many people were still thinking like teen me, but there were much bigger issues at play than one transsexual wanting his passport to say *Miss.*

The thought that women can have their rights engulfed by a parade of bored teens who fancy being a bit spicy before settling down to 2.5 kids and a mortgage really pissed me off. So now I am logical and open about what I think. Of course trans people have a right to exist and lead a happy life free from harm - but so do women. I think sex is paramount over gender when it comes to women and men.

My daughters have needed to avoid being pulled into the trans whirlpool at school and thankfully they do listen to their mum and are happy and confident in being young women. Long may it last. I trust common sense will prevail and people just take time to think - and thought is the light that Stonewall would prefer we didn't shine on the messages it is pushing.

* * * *

Anon

84

Wax on, wax off

The moment I became aware of Gender Critical views was the case of Jessica Yaniv from British Columbia in 2019.

Until this point, it had all passed me by, until I realised that this man, who self-identified as a women, expected those poor beauticians to shave his balls!

What a bloody cheek, thank goodness he lost the tribunal. I remember this case triggered a big family discussion over it, as my daughter-in-law is a beautician, and we were all gobsmacked.

• • • •

Anon

85

What this TERF has to say

To start, I'm a biracial, and bisexual woman. I'm currently 24. For years upon years I very much advocated for the idea that 'Transwomen are women! And transmen are men! Non-binary is real!' Despite all this, I still acknowledged biological sex. The only drawback to that was I did buy in to the 'female and male brain'. I had expressed views that weren't always considered 'TERF rhetoric', such as 'You can't have a period without a uterus'. I even did mental gymnastics that 'TW can be lesbians, but AMAB (assigned male at birth) non-binaries can't be'.

This did get me into debates after a few years as the rhetoric from gender ideology evolved. At the time I felt like LGBT was the whole acronym, that asexuals aren't inherently part of the group just because they lack sexual attraction. I was a battle-axe bisexual so I felt (and still feel) that 'pansexuality' is just a more woke version of bisexuality (for lack of a better term). I agreed that asexuals could be part of the community based on romantic attraction, but if they weren't attracted to the same gender (as I put it then) and if they weren't trans, they weren't LGBT.

I didn't throw my hat into the ring of whether or not I was in the same camp as *transmeds*, or *tucutes*, because to me I felt I wasn't trans and it, therefore, wasn't my place to have a say in that debate. I followed those kinds of account on Twitter, which I didn't use often at the time, I still use it the least out of all my social medias. But I did open it one day and saw one of the 'anti-biphobia' accounts I followed sharing a, very obvious, joke from a lesbian calling some bisexuals 'dick-worshippers'. Being that I'm a fan of self-deprecating humour, I clicked on the tweet itself, and saw she was talking about bisexual women who had never dated women, merely talked about the fact that they can.

Aside from self-deprecation, I didn't have fond feelings towards my own community, mostly the online community. I felt (and still feel) that bisexuality is the easiest sexuality to claim for the sake of being 'different'. Like being same-sex attracted (or again as I called it, same gender) was some sort of quirky club for people to join.

Back to the main point, I clicked on the woman's profile to look at the other tweets she'd made, because what she said made me laugh, so I wanted to see her other posts. I immediately saw 'radfem' in her bio. So I thought to myself, "Geez, here we go. Let's see what this TERF has to say".
The more I read however, the more I saw that I agreed with. I'm a former kinkster. And frankly, I went along with kinks to please my mentally-abusive ex-boyfriend. I had convinced myself that I was also into these things, but after a while I realized I just used that as a cover. I wasn't into *CNC*. I didn't like being choked. But it made him happy, and if I said no he would be mad.
She had those kinds of tweets. Tweets against prostitution, about the exploitation that is surrogacy, and so many things I heavily agreed with. The only thing I didn't agree with at the time, was being against transgenderism. So I made a private list of radical feminists on twitter - I didn't really want to follow them, but I did want to hear what they had to say. After all, you can agree with people you normally disagree with.

Over time I looked more into what radical feminism was about, but I still wanted to be inclusive of transwomen. A few months in that changed for me. Before I had peaked, before I had actually read what radfems believed in, the people in my circles would agree that 'genital preference' wasn't inherently transphobic. But now, all of a sudden there were people who were saying it was: in large waves I noticed this. It was odd to me and shocking, because I went from a space where it was rarely discussed, and when it was there was no issue, to it now being 'literal violence' and 'bigotry'.
For a short while I started to believe in the concept of 'True trans'. I peaked when I saw a woman discussing her rape, the offender being a transwoman. They told her she was lying, and those who didn't laughed at her about it. I peaked there. I peaked even more when I saw rape and death threats. After all of this I finally read the essay JKR had written, and thought; "This? This is what makes her a TERF? This is somehow inciting violence against their community?"

More and more I saw the stereotypes they participated in,

I saw they had no regard for boundaries and more. I have sympathy for the transmen and transwomen who are 'straight'. How horrible it must be to think your attraction to the same sex is abnormal, to think you have to try changing your sex because of it. I feel for many transmen who believe that because they aren't feminine they must not be women. I truly believe those who try to enforce strict gender roles on their children have failed their children. Boys can play with dolls, girls can play with GI Joes. And while they say that, "Clothes don't make you trans, hobbies and interests don't make you trans," they force trans on any gender non-compliant person. Even historical figures. Women who spoke up and fought for other women are now seen as 'non-binary' or 'they were actually transwomen'.

I couldn't support that movement anymore. I can't. I do believe they deserve rights, but male access to women's spaces is not a right. Cosmetic surgery that leaves these people being life long medical patients for life is not a right. Access to lesbians and gay men, sleeping with them, is not a right.

What they're asking for are *privileges*.

• • • •

Anon

Enter Mumsnet!

I was vaguely aware of the debate, and was of the view that I didn't mind who I shared my spaces with. Trans people were small in number and I didn't see how it could turn into a big issue.

In walks Mumsnet!

On a thread about changing rooms I wrote a comment stating my view that I didn't care sharing my space with men or trans people. It was very quickly pointed out that I might not care but others did, and I could not give away the rights of others. I realised how short-sighted I'd been in only thinking about myself, and no one else, so I decided that I was going to educate myself on what others thought. For this I came to Twitter.

I started following everyone that had something to say on the matter. I started noticing very quickly, however, that I was getting almost instantly blocked by almost everyone on one side of the debate. What this showed me, someone trying to learn and understand, was that one side didn't want someone who thought. The red flags went up.

So thank you to all those that blocked me, you opened my eyes to what was truly going on, and left me surrounded by other free-thinking, gender critical folk.

• • • •

Anon

87

I didn't want to be a coward

I'm a young GC woman (23 years old), which is quite difficult considering the prevalence of TRA ideology among my generation. I used to be a TRA myself as a teenager, preaching about how puberty blockers are good and males in female spaces aren't dangerous and all that sort of nonsense. My friends and I would sometimes read 'TERF' content on social media just to laugh at it rather than critically examine it.

But one day, I saw a post on a 'TERF' Tumblr blog containing a list of males who had committed sex crimes in women's bathrooms, and this actually made me stop and think. It made me do this because, only the previous day, I had read a left-wing media article confidently asserting that these types of crimes 'never happen'. The media had evidently lied to me about this, so I started wondering what else they had lied to me about.

Once I let go of my naivety and started looking into the facts, the whole ideology fell apart. I had stupidly believed that the mainstream media wouldn't tell outright lies, so I had blindly trusted their assertions that, "Trans people are murdered for being trans" (not in the UK); "Predatory men would never pretend to be trans women" (they do all the time); and "No-one ever regrets transitioning" (many young people do).

Once I saw the hard evidence that these assertions weren't true, I couldn't in good conscience continue being a TRA. Another thing which helped me break TRA conditioning was that I knew what it felt like to be disbelieved. I had been in an emotionally abusive relationship and eventually broken up with my abuser, but because he was better at manipulating people to sympathise with him, all my friends picked his side and abandoned me. I didn't want to be a coward like them.

When I heard women presenting evidence that TRA ideology was making them suffer, I believed them. I just feel ashamed that

I didn't try to seek out those women's voices sooner, and instead I listened to the left-wing media, which drowned out GC viewpoints.

This all happened a few years ago and it's amazing to see how much progress has been made in such a short time. Everyone gets to hear our side of the story now, and I can only hope that more women of my generation start waking up to the truth.

• • • •

Anon

88

A dent in my certainties

2018. Squashed into the tiny Women's Tent at the *Green Gathering Festival*. Hot, largely unaware, and determined to 'be kind'. I listened to two women who worked at a rape crisis centre, terrified at the potential loss of women-only services. An older lesbian spoke of the disappearance of her community, an eco-activist raised concerns about the take-over of the movement; a mother was fearful for her young daughter.

I say 'I listened', but somehow – to my shame - I didn't hear. Maybe it all seemed too ridiculous; maybe I was scared to actually join the dots; maybe I didn't dare to acknowledge the extent to which society will always prioritise men's desires over women's human rights. And how little we matter. Certainly I hung on for grim death to my sense of self as compassionate, tolerant, empathetic, and kind. Always bloody kind.

But an (almost imperceptible) dent had been made in my certainties. As more and more women spoke out, the inadequacy of kindness as a response to the witch-hunts, threats and public shaming they endured, became increasingly evident.

Nonetheless, I continued to try. I talked of compromises, third-spaces, mutual misunderstandings. I wrote to politicians to ask if they would please consider allowing vulnerable women to have female-only services. I objected – politely – to men being allowed to compete against women on the sports' field. I suggested that it was inappropriate for men to stand, and be accepted, as Women's Officers in political parties.
I truly thought that once the people making these decisions understood the impact on women, they would rush to put things right. (*I know, I know.*)

Then in 2019 the dent turned in to a bomb crater. I was contributing to a thread on Mumsnet about single-sex spaces.

Kindness, empathy and compromise abounded as we collectively tried to find a way of balancing male demands and women's safety.

Exploding into the middle of this conversation came a woman on the run in the USA from her violently abusive husband, camping out in car parks and forests with her young child. She was eloquent, angry and absolutely desperate. The nearest women-only shelter was almost 2,000 miles away (it has since been forced to admit men) and she had no way of getting to it. Even asking for women-only provision had led to her being called a bigot and a gender essentialist by the very people who were suppose to help her.

It was a Damascene moment. I'm just sorry it took me so long.

• • • •

Anon

89

I saw womanhood as a club

I peaked when a friend of mine, one of my dearest friends actually, started feeling the need to follow me around on Facebook adding disclaimers whenever I commented in any conversation on trans identity. What jarred me was that at that stage - more than five years ago - I was still earning the wrath of more seasoned gender critical feminists for tiptoeing around my stale idea of TiMs as forlorn, frail, disassociated and tormented souls who needed my girlfriendly welcome by having me call them 'she' and 'her.' I thought of it as a kind of intimate exception which didn't affect anybody for real.

I'd not heard of *AGP* nor seen the disgusting, porny savagery of its view of women as mere *f*ckable holes* - holes one can *become*. So at that point I was at pains to nurse my cognitive dissonance in order to be 'polite' to men at women's expense, and my dear friend's need to publicly disassociate herself from 'Cathoel and her disgusting views' hurt me deeply.

This friend was about fifteen years older than me and I suspect she may have had to overleap some repulsion in her own heart... and leapt too far. She seemed driven by the fear of exclusion and being called 'old and past it' - which, as we now see, was prescient. Two years after our parting I wrote to her, saying I miss you so much, can we get past this. She sent back such a shrivelling, pious little lecture that all desire to reunite with her died an acid death.

I wrote her a letter in reply which I later published:

https://houseoflovers.com/literature/this-racist-homophobic-cult/

It rather shames me now that I was still seeing womanhood as a cosy club which women are obliged to welcome stray souls into. That I had bought into the rather gross fantasy of the women's bathrooms as a gossipy hub for tampon sharing rather than a private space where women take a deep breath away from the toxic, near-universal, loaded air of patriarchal threat. I was living then in Berlin, perhaps the most sexually transgressive city on earth, and it was a shock to see the lesbian march infested with gynophobic banners.

• • • •

Anon

90

Exhausted, stressed and fearful

I work in a university, teaching gender and women's studies (started when gender was about stereotypes, not a religion demanding belief in sex change). If I had your courage and was open, students would claim to feel 'unsafe' and, although I doubt I would be sacked (strong labour laws and work with decent people), I would be removed from teaching and unable to publish, and women's studies would certainly end completely.

I was completely in the 'be kind' camp until about 2016-2017. I had a few nagging doubts, but thought trans women were usually effeminate gay men who suffered oppression. I was beginning to wonder why all the trans women I knew, however, were heterosexual. I was getting 'friendly reminders' about pronouns and so on, and going along with it, no problem. Then I saw a piece on a feminist forum where a feminist noted that biologically intact males were being placed in women's prisons under the label of identity. What shocked me even more than this information, was the pile on the feminist experienced from other so-called feminists. Misgendering rapists was a crime equivalent to the holocaust, according to these people... and some even insisted that (biological) women were as capable of sex crimes as men, and as likely to commit them, it was just that gender stereotyping meant they were under the radar. I couldn't believe what I was reading... *wtf???*

I think that peaked me, but I 'zombied' along. Then, on another feminist forum, this one for academics, a woman sought advice for her ten-year-old daughter who was 'trans' - woman seemed very proud of it - and needed gender-affirming care. Forum was trans friendly so full of trans women - and trans men, who, although 'triggered' by 'breast-feeding' seemed ok to be on a 'women's forum'. An *ingénue* from a discipline that probably hadn't encountered much of this waded in and suggested that perhaps the little girl was suffering from other issues that could be explored, such as difficulties in adolescence. Not for one moment did she say there was anything wrong in being trans, just that there might be other stuff going on as well. I knew at that stage that the pile-on would occur immediately, and I was right. The woman was accused by two trans women of spreading transphobic myths. I defended the *ingénue* and left the forum. As I was on it under my real name I still feared doxing and that my name is stored somewhere.

    I am exhausted, stressed and fearful. In the academy now, there are vast expanses of human history and thought that cannot be mentioned, bibliographies that cannot be included, topics that cannot be raised. Meanwhile, the same patriarchal bulls**** is oppressing women and girls everywhere, and we can't even discuss it without a zillion caveats to include the multiple gender identities apparently possible…

• • • •

Anon

The cotton ceiling

In 2018 I went to London Pride.

I had not been in years because it had gotten too corrupt and straight. Anyway, I went and heard about the protests at the start of the march. I didn't see it, I was just told a bunch of 'bigots and TERFs' had been protesting… that was my first time hearing the word 'TERF'.

The next day I decided to Google what happened and I found that the group protesting was *'Get the L Out'* so I found a podcast with Angela Wild about the *cotton ceiling* and that is when I realised people actually believed TWAW (transwomen are women) and that lesbians and women in general should accept them as women.

The rest is history.

• • • •

Aja

92

A chilling response

There were dozens of small issues that made no sense or made me uncomfortable. Eventually my best friend very tentatively probed my views and I realised I wasn't alone.

Then I met a young person who had initially expressed a wish to transition but now seemed reluctant. I put out a tweet to other people to identify a local non-directive counsellor.

The response I received was chilling.

If I didn't immediately send them to a therapist who would affirm them, they would commit suicide and it would be my fault. It was the first time I'd heard the great myth, so I was horrified. I closed my account and it was a long time before I returned.

Now I'm back, I don't give a stuff: I'm not going to be manipulated and intimidated like that again, so if a TRA is talking nonsense, I'll tell them so, sometimes politely and respectfully and sometimes a little more *shoutily*.

• • • •

Anon

Steppin' out over the line

My first inkling of a 'trans rights vs. women's rights' issue was the controversy over Bruce Springsteen's trans-inclusive women's washroom policy at his 2016 concerts. I remember ignorantly thinking, "Hmm, what's all the fuss about?" It took another three years for me to wake up. By then I'd heard a few voices on social media describe the comedy-writer Graham Linehan as being 'transphobic'. Puzzled, I tuned into a conversation between Linehan and Benjamin Boyce where this charge was debunked within minutes. This led me to watch more Boyce interviews, notably Meghan Murphy, who'd not only been monstered but permanently suspended from Twitter. She made loads of sense and I was disturbed by the accounts she was giving, similar to Linehan's, of children being medicalised and receiving 'affirmative' surgery; about women's refuges being closed down in Canada by a powerful trans lobby group. I confess I initially shut the medicalisation and surgery stuff out of my brain. I found it too difficult to process; too horrific to be possible in 2019, surely?

In the Youtube side-bar was a video entitled 'What Kind of Fools Do Transgender UK and Stonewall Take Us For?' by someone called Magdalen Berns. This video and another by Berns from 2017 - concerning the violent assault of Maria MacLachlan by a trans-identifying male - were what tipped me over the edge, as did the lack of outrage at this attack on MacLachlan and the assault of Julie Bindel in 2019. Why hadn't I heard about these two incidents on news bulletins or in the papers? Call a woman a 'TERF' and suddenly you could dehumanize her, behave however you wanted and dismiss crimes perpetrated against her.

I still hid my concerns from my friends and family, as I knew somebody whose child had dysphoria, although not well enough to feel I could raise my concerns. I also noticed that lots of U.K. stand-up comedians, who I'd previously admired for being discerning and well-read, were either completely silent on this issue or were lazily parroting TRA rhetoric and calling the LGB Alliance a 'hate group'. A handful of Labour MPs were following suit. I very quickly felt politically homeless. What finally emboldened me to speak out on social media - and to the captive audience of my Instagram followers - was when I heard Aaron Kimberly, a Canada-based transman and mental health clinician, tell Benjamin Boyce about the bullying and silencing of dissenting transpeople.

I resolved to only retweet posts by trans and detrans voices so that my friends and family could see how destructive gender-identity ideology was, without mistaking me for a bigot. This totally backfired, as both a friend and my own sibling got in contact to tell me that I was a bigot and a conspiracy theorist. I was also accused of 'punching down' for mocking *Pink News'* headline about 'queer hikers proving the great outdoors isn't just for cis, straight, middle class folk'.

"Why is a middle-aged, white cis man concerned with trans and queer people?!" asked my sibling. The friend's parting shot was to tell me that sex was 'a spectrum'.

I realised how uninformed most people were, especially if they relied on *The Guardian* or *Radio 4.*

• • • •

Ally

94

This is not how we should treat children

In about 1986 I read Invisible Women by Dale Spender. It blew me away. It explained why I, a female, had been ignored throughout my school life and introduced me to feminism. I then read more and more books about how girls and women are conditioned to be quiet, take up no space, centre males and generally look after males. I read mainly books relating to education as I was a primary school teacher at the time.

One of the most shocking facts discovered through my reading was that girls get 35% of any teachers' time and boys, therefore, get 65%. We did an experiment in my class to disprove this: the data showed definite 35% / 65% split. Even though the children were actively involved in the research the boys were not happy when we tried to make it a 36% / 64% split.

As a result of this bit of action research I decided to delve further into the murky world of sexism in school. I was lucky, at the time there were many resources available. Even the government (Conservative) had realised there was sexism in schools and produced Genderwatch while it was people in many Labour constituencies who produced wonderful resources for use in schools.

I used many of the resources I found in my classroom and watched both girls and boys blossom. It relieved the boys of having to be alpha males and allowed the girls to be intelligent and play football. I met a lot of resistance from other staff, both male and female. The head teacher appeared to support me, asking me to write their Equal Opportunities Policy; a policy based on combating sexism/racism/ablism. I did this. However, when I asked him to actually follow the policy I had written he asked me to leave. (I did and got a higher level job).

In all my jobs I continued to try and eradicate the sexism inherent in teaching. I learnt to be a bit more subtle, but students continued to appreciate being allowed to break out of the boxes sexist stereotyping had placed them in.

    Scroll forward to 2012 or 2013. I was teaching adults by now. I had a group of females and males who I had been teaching for a few months. The group really gelled. Then 'Kate' arrived (I have changed his name). 'Kate' was built like a brickhouse door, stomped rather than walked, wore beautiful (expensive) wigs and clothes designed for women. I had been given some warning by my manager and told 'Kate' was a man transitioning to become a woman. I believed what I was told. I called 'Kate' by female pronouns, even correcting other staff when they called 'Kate' 'he', or were disrespectful.

    Though I tried my best I couldn't understand how a man could just decide he was a woman and asked the college counsellor about it. She told me it was all to do with how 'Kate' felt. I was still confused but went along with it because I had no other points of reference to explain 'Kate'.

'Kate' was continually disruptive in class. Constantly talking loudly on his mobile, while refusing to engage with any of the other students. He totally changed the atmosphere in the room. My female students and I took to going to the toilets on another floor in the building so they would not meet 'Kate' in the Ladies. At the time I wasn't on Facebook. Tutors were discouraged from being on Facebook, or if they were on it from allowing students to be their friends on it. 'Kate' kept emailing me (at my college address) asking me to friend him on Facebook. I did look at his page, all his friends were males who claimed to be women too.

    Eventually 'Kate's' disruption got to the point where I had to do something more than try deal with it in the classroom. I spoke to him privately and asked him to be less disruptive. He immediately called me transphobic and reported me to HR. Absolutely taking no responsibility for his own behaviour. HR and my line manager spoke to me. Luckily this was 2013, transgender ideology had not taken such a hold on education establishments, plus I had written evidence of every one of 'Kate's' disruptions which I had regularly passed on to my boss, and I was the one in the department who had done any sexism/racism/disability training (my line manager was used to me picking colleagues up on any signs of sexism/racism/ableism).

    Both HR and my line manager listened to my side of what

had gone on and agreed there was no further action needed. 'Kate' then left to do a course on some form of female beauty course in a different building. The last I heard was he was asked to leave the college.

Before 'Kate' the whole issue of transgender ideology had passed me by. After 'Kate' I began to try and find out about it. It immediately became clear to me that transgender ideology is the total opposite of Equal Opportunities. Transgender ideology stops children from experimenting, from growing, from understanding about sexism and how it affects their lives. Transgender ideology is a harmful regressive ideology which allows males like 'Kate' to invade women's spaces. I fight against transgender ideology because my heart goes out to all the girls who want to play football and the boys who like pink who in the 1980s were encouraged to be full human beings who would now be told there is something wrong with them. This is not how we should treat children.

I finally realised the whole premise is fundamentally flawed - and I started off pretty neutral. Transwomen were people who had a very difficult mental health problem and needed adjustments within society to help them live their lives. I didn't really give it much thought, if I'm honest. It never affected me, or anyone I knew.

And then I got a job as PSHE (personal, social, health and economic education) lead in a new school. I need this to stay anonymous for that reason - my social media account is pretty terfy and very left wing, and I can't be political given my profession. Kids need to know I'm someone who they can rely on to be fair, regardless of their political persuasion.

As PSHE lead I needed to update the school schemes of work, particularly given the changes at the time. It was about two years before statutory RSE (relationships and sex education) was coming into force. So I started looking at our resources, and those available from reputable sources (such as Stonewall and the PSHE Association). And I imagined the range of teenage responses (because in asking others to actually teach I needed to pre-empt difficult questions). I started questioning from a critical position. But *why* are some people born in the wrong body, and *how* does that happen? It was clear almost immediately that these questions could not be answered unless we relied on stereotypes or junk science.

As a science teacher, the idea that the mind and body are entirely separate entities was never going to wash - our brains *are part of* our bodies, we are not separate entities, so we cannot be born in the wrong one. We are also expressly forbidden from reinforcing stereotypes about men and women. I became completely lost. It felt like there was no way to teach this without talking nonsense about 'lady-brain' or using stereotypes. As a female physics teacher (former engineer) I'm never going to give in to those nonsense ideas. So I finally realised that the whole premise is fundamentally flawed.

Nobody is 'born in the wrong body'. There is no such thing as a 'womanly essence' or a 'gendered soul'. Some people believe it, that's fine. Lots of people believe in God, but I'd never teach that as a fact! Similarly, I absolutely will never either believe in gendered souls, nor teach them as fact. Then I started looking more critically at the 'reputable' resources I'd assumed were okay. I had previous experience working in building design and so was pretty well-versed in the difference between legislation, statutory guidance and generic advice. And the 'competence' of those who often write the latter.

My scrutiny of resources found that many were contradictory to the statutory guidance/legislation and the rest were dubious at best. I ended up quitting the PSHE lead post because I could not find a sensible way forward. From there, I became aware of the wider ramifications of gender identity theory, and the damage done to women's rights. Mumsnet was invaluable in this - fairly open moderation so I can be exposed to a range of ideas without too much censorship.

I'm still not as active as I would like, and I hope that will change. For now, I'm limited to writing to my MP, answering honestly the questions my students ask, and donating to fundraisers. I have noticed a shift though. About a year ago I plucked up the courage to contradict the Brooke advisory on a ridiculous talk they gave. The new PSHE lead had moaned to the deputy head about my (very polite) contradictory email, but the deputy head agreed with everything I said.

Brooke promised to update their material with the correct scientific facts, PSHE lessons went over the incorrect stuff and fixed it, and I'm now asked to review our 'trans' resources for scientific accuracy and political bias. There is still so much more though. I teach a couple of trans/non-binary children and I've always used preferred pronouns and names (after checking parents are aware - I take a strict opposition to supporting social transition without parents' knowledge). But after reading the interim Cass review I'm worried that even this is risky to the children.

I don't know what more to do. Deliberately misgendering is potentially harassment and I want children to feel comfortable in my classroom, as that helps their learning. But affirming a trans identity might actually harm the child. Teachers are not psychologists, psychiatrists, gender identity clinicians. This is well beyond the scope of our expertise. We desperately need clear, unequivocal and scientifically sound advice.

• • • •

Anon

95

Reality denied

Social Housing, London 2011. Women-only. A TIM (trans-identifying male) is put in the adjacent studio (a conversion, think 'rooms in a Victorian boarding house'). He's 'emotionally Interesting' as they call it in the Simpsons, but then, so am I. I'll call him Dana International (he lives in the EU most of the year). I treat him as a female. This proves to be unwise.

Short version of a very long story. He had fits of explosive rage; an attempt to kick in my door, kicks holes in the corridor wall. I understood that the authorities could do little about my subjective claims but the denial of an objective fact alarmed me. A male mammal had been placed in protective housing for female mammals but it could not (pre-Forstater) be mentioned and therefore could not be addressed. The language I needed to describe reality was denied me.

I'm lucky. I have a brain and the brothers I grew up fighting with, who fitted deadbolts and a spy-hole and projected their male voices through the partition wall to send an extraordinarily retrograde message that shouldn't have been needed in 2011, "This female has male relatives who will physically protect her from males. From you."

NB; A female attempting to kick-in the door to my 'cave', wouldn't have traumatised me, triggered my 'freeze' response, fired the fear circuits in my limbic system (physical shocks went up & down my spine). I'm a fighter not a lover. I can protect myself from a woman. I can't protect myself from a man. It took me years to get over it.

I'm fine now, but fully peaked. What about women in prisons and hostels (I was in one for three years) without my advantages? Why are people in authority lying about material reality? Why are institutions lying about the physical differences between the sex evolved for explosive strength in combat and the sex evolved for childbirth? About the differences in offending patterns being sex specific but, unsurprisingly, unaffected by gender identity. By words.

Why are only trans-identifying men considered for mixed-sex prisons but not left-handed or short-sighted men when all have the same bodies, pose the same risk, induce the same fear, pack the same punch? Why do males have a single-sex prison option but not females? How did the language in the GRA get passed by government lawyers? (Where are the definitions of sex and gender 'for the purposes of this Act'?) Why are the younger sons of the aristocracy explicitly protected from their elder sisters inheriting their father's title ('The Horror! The Horror!') but not women from sharing prisons with men? How can we safely afford males female levels of access to females and infants when rape and paedophilia are almost uniquely male behaviours?

Why are the GMC saying 'sex assigned at birth' when my neighbours' cat knows sex is observed and recorded, not to mention immutable and decided at conception? Why are they asking for my meaningless *legal sex* but not my vital biological sex?

Why are otherwise intelligent people pretending a GRC means anything more, CAN mean anything more, than that a holder can lie about his biological sex without committing fraud? Notwithstanding the shameful obfuscation in the GRA (Laws are meant to make order out of chaos, not create it) this much is clear. Both biological males and biological females, have the legal sex male and vice versa. Thus all sex markers on documents, issued post-2004, are meaningless as evidence of biological sex, be it for India Willoughby or Princess Charlotte. Everyone's biological sex is concealed within a new meaningless category - *legal sex* - to afford privacy to people whose gender identity differs from their biological sex. No mammal has changed biological sex. And the logical impossibility of 'Schrödinger's single-sex spaces' and *de facto* self-ID means there is really only one question. Which sex-segregated spaces are we now designating mixed-sex?

The 'how' of this madness is becoming clear; the capture of our institutions via the once noble mechanisms already in place; e.g; the secret 'training' by a lobby group corrupting the ETBB (Equal Treatment Bench Book). Judge James Taylor cited it in his erroneous Forstater judgement; a book that is no more the Law than the Argos catalogue. Terrifying. I expect 'Gendered Intelligence' to play the BBC for fools. But Judges?

The 'why' is complex and fascinating and will become clearer to future historians as totalitarian periods always do. We humans code for truth. This too shall pass. But we need to fight to keep the Enlightenment. We always have and some of us haven't forgotten how.

And for me Ovid's aphorism is proving surprisingly true.

Happy are those who dare courageously to defend what they love.

. . . .

Anon

96

Alienated

I feel utterly alienated from left wing politics. I was born into a liberal, intellectual Jewish family, the middle child of three siblings, the only girl between two noisy, disruptive brothers; it was only much later that I understood that my role was to be the 'easy one'. My brothers' Bar Mitzvahs were grand, important affairs which marked their change in role within the community so that they could now read from the Torah during services. As a girl, I had always been segregated from the men and taken no active role in the services. My Bat Chayil was a much smaller affair shared with other girls.

I was aware of the discrepancy in roles and of conflict caused by the expectation that my Mum would perform the multiple domestic roles expected of a Jewish wife. I was interested in social injustice and was keen to study Sociology at O-level and A-level but it was only when I went to Birmingham Poly in 1984 that I discovered feminism. It hit me like a bolt out the blue and changed me viscerally; it made sense of so many things and released a rage inside me which was impossible to contain.

I became involved in campaigns against pornography and sexual harassment; I became aware of Justice for Women and the campaigns to release women from life sentences for murdering their abusive husbands; I marched against David Alton's proposed Bill to reduce abortion rights. I went to NUS Women's Conference and was profoundly inspired by being at such a large event by women for women focused on women's experience of our oppression. I remember vividly reading Andrea Dworkin's book 'Pornography' and feeling so fired up by her words. However, I was aware of a feeling of disappointment at the end when the author didn't seem to me to be pointing to a solution or a way forward.

I became interested in left wing politics and discovered a revolutionary Marxist group which recognised the importance of self-organisation by oppressed groups such as women and understood the central importance of these struggles. Their approach was different to other similar groups like the SWP and Militant which were vehemently against self-organisation and prioritised class struggle above all others. I saw the importance of a radical socialist overhaul of society as the way forward for women's liberation.

I spent the next 30 years actively involved in numerous left wing and progressive campaigns: anti-racism, anti-war, Palestine solidarity, anti-apartheid, anti-austerity etc., and regrettably lost touch with my feminist activism although never with my feminist beliefs. I was actively involved in the campaign to get Jeremy Corbyn elected in my local Labour Party when the GRA Consultation began. I began to read about it and was hugely concerned about the threat that reform of this legislation presented to women's sex-based rights.

I anxiously, but determinedly, attended the first *A Woman's Place* public meeting in Manchester on my own, terrified that it would be picketed and that the speakers would be full of hate. To my joy it wasn't; it was packed to the rafters with glorious women fighting to defend our sex-based rights. I felt completely affirmed in my fears about what was being proposed regarding the GRA, but I remained highly anxious about speaking out. The local LP Women's Forum agreed without discussion that it would be open to anyone who 'identifies' as a woman so I thought I was completely alone. I carried this fear for many weeks before a chance remark to a fellow female Corbynista thankfully linked me with other women in the Branch who felt the same way I did.

We linked up and began posting on the Corbyn-supporting Facebook page articles exposing the attack on women and same sex attracted people of transactivism. We were immediately attacked as 'transphobes' and articles taken down without discussion. It was devastating for me to experience the speed and ease with which men I had thought of as my comrades embraced this vicious ideology. This devastation remains with me today and I feel utterly alienated from left wing politics even though I remain a socialist at heart. Now, my feminist politics are my top priority, and I will do all in my power to help defeat transactivism.

* * * *

Anon

Radicalised for the first time

Back in 2018 a friend who works for the local council sent me a USA video of a boy beating girls in what was clearly an all-girls race. I found it both absurd and preposterous. I was told, "This is happening now". We got talking and I fell down the 'self-identification' rabbit hole. She discovered that our local education authority (LEA) was proposing to introduce what it called a 'Transgender Toolkit'; no consultation with parents. We reviewed it. It was anonymously-authored; no credentials to check; written in chilling, compulsory language inappropriate for a sensitive policy on the care of infant school age children upwards. It directed schools to let boys use any girls' facilities without question (despite The Times Educational Supplement publishing an article in 2017 on what it called the 'epidemic' of sexual harassment of girls by boys in schools). It directed teachers to diagnose very young children as 'probably trans', if they played with toys that didn't match the applicable sex-based stereotype. It misrepresented, or simply ignored, the law.

Apparently, this policy had been passed by the safeguarding board. I knew nothing about Education policy or LEA duties. My friend had to stay anonymous because the County Council is her employer. 18 months of persistent challenging and explaining the law followed. Finally the LEA withdrew it 'for review'. As far as I know, we were the first parents in the UK to challenge an LEA on its transgender policies. Then we found out about *Fair Play For Women* and started attending secret meetings in London and Birmingham and *A Woman's Place* in Oxford, meeting soon-to-be Resistance luminaries such as Dr Jane Clare Jones, Maya Forstater and Dr Nic Williams.

We got out on the streets leafleting and campaigning for *Fair Play for Women*. My friend went on to co-found *Safe Schools Alliance*. I am a keen amateur athlete and turned my attention to sport, now challenging national governing bodies as part of the

Women's Rights Network sports group.

I challenged policy at the Solicitors Regulation Authority with *Sex Matters* and *Legal Feminist* co-founder, Rebecca Bull. I was also at the first meeting of what was to become *Legal Feminist* (Advocates Assemble!) but stepped back due to a big dose of imposter syndrome.

When people asked me how I was going to celebrate turning 50, I had no idea the answer was, "Becoming politically radicalised for the first time in my life".

• • • •

Anon

98

Throwing his weight around

I left a 'cockfrocker' 20 years ago, well before it was 'fashionable'.

It took me years to get over it and it was in silence. There were no *"Yaaaas kweeeen!"* supporters back then, and I went to therapy alone. It was Gavin 'Manslab Hit-and-Run Driver' Blubbard that peaked me and made me inquire further - being in New Zealand and seeing his massive balding frame and his Neanderthal-like skulldome.

He was colonising women's weight-lifting here, and a wonderful, dainty little TERF from the UK was making waves with her unapologetic stance towards men in dresses being called women. I saved my disposable income and bought a 'Woman: Adult Human Female' t-shirt from her, and I bless Posie Parker every day since.

I've been lucky enough to have been interviewed by her since then, and my stance has become even MORE adamantine.

. . . .

Ngā mihi!

Rex Landy,
TERF, Professional Nobody

99

Can you live with yourself?

Perhaps you can remember 1994. Perhaps you, like me, can remember bits of 1994, but a lot of it is, let's say, slightly 'hazy'. At the time of writing, 1994 is fast-approaching 30 years ago. No matter when you are reading this though, 1994 will doubtless seem like a long time before the beginning of Gender Identity Ideology, and the rise of the Trans Rights Activist. Despite all of this, it's when my story truly begins.

    I am ending my teens and entering my twenties. For as long as I can remember, I've lived with a deep-seated unhappiness, a sense of being outcast in social circles and 'unwanted' in the home. The memories of standing stock still and solitary in the playground aged five, staring blankly at the walls or the ground, frozen by this unhappiness, are among my earliest. My 20-year-old self is looking back over how life thus far has been - chased by a cloud of sadness, overcompensating to be the classroom joker who's always ready with a clever retort has become the default setting.

    It serves as a useful shield, keeping prying questions at bay. I don't know how to express myself in front of people, but I have become very proficient musically, which allowed me some emotional outlet at least. Now, I'm an adult. I've got my first proper job. The orchestra work is no more, the rock bands have given way to electronic music made in bedrooms instead of rehearsal rooms. And I've grown a belly.

    Me? But I've always been so slim, so trim, so SKINNY! It's one of my most recognisable traits: over-tall and underweight. It seems that all that work blowing wind instruments must have been keeping my stomach flat. "Well, I can't play as much any more, but I have been eating extra burgers and chips quite a lot lately, so I'll cut down on them."

    So, I do. But somehow, at this seemingly innocent moment, my perception is skewed. No matter how much I cut down on the food, the belly seems to be getting bigger and bigger. A storm has brewed without my awareness. I have an abusive life in the parental home, I can't cope with the massive changes that becoming an adult brings, and I've noticed a change in my body. I need to control something, ANYTHING. I can't change my father, and I need to earn money, so... the food. The food has to go.

Body dysmorphia must take many forms, I'm sure. My experience may be quite typical, or not. I don't know. I can only share with you how it was, and why it matters.

For me, there were none of the typical influences that were very prominent at the time. I was not influenced by magazines, inspired by music videos, or put under peer pressure. I was caught in a spiral of mental ill health. It became very powerful, very quickly. I lost all understanding of why fuelling the body was important to stay alive. Seriously – I didn't understand why I needed to eat and poo. That nonsense was for other people.

There was a health and fitness drive at work, which included a physical assessment. I had my body fat measured, and it came in at under 5%. I was very proud to have the lowest score of the group, but also unhappy that it was only the same as elite athletes, and not lower. In the space of only 3 months, I lost 50 pounds.

The psychological pain of dysphoria is hard to express. The experience of body dysmorphia is perhaps easier. Looking at my body, I saw what was not there. By which I mean that I actually, physically perceived it. It's very much like an hallucination, but entirely convincing and believable - maybe because it's at least based on a reality. My eyes must have captured the image of a tortured body in starvation, wasting further away with every day, but my brain saw swollen fatness. The experience wasn't even uncomfortable, because I didn't know I wasn't observing the real world. This was the dysmorphia. An absolute submission of the senses giving way to the illness, showing my brain that which was not true, which was not real.

But the emotional response was violent and visceral. I was GROTESQUE! I was an ABOMINATION! Other people must be DISGUSTED by me! How could I even be worthy of having a body if I could allow it to become so bloated. This was the dysphoria, the inner demon of self-loathing. God damn, I hate that demon so much.

It took a conversation with my best friend to break the spell. She was leaving for university at the end of the summer, and I was facing losing another thing in my life that I dearly loved. The last time we spoke before she packed, she told me in no uncertain terms that I was going to die if I carried on this way. It was such a shock.

I'd never considered it before, because I believed I was losing weight and being healthy, because being fat is unhealthy, and look at how massive and gross I am! Somehow though, the message got through. She saved my life that day.

Fast forward 20 years, to 2014. I am recovered. All but the smallest vestiges of anorexia are behind me. I still find it very uncomfortable eating in company. Very rarely, I experience body dysmorphia too, but now I have enough awareness to spot it coming and let it pass, like a wave. Most often when it comes now, it's when I look at my hands. I see my hand in front of me, growing and growing like that scene from *An American Werewolf in London*. Yes, I'm thankful it doesn't happen very often any more!

In the time that has elapsed, I flirted with spirituality before putting that aside and become a sceptic. Not a cynic, but someone who engages in critical thinking. My sceptical hero is James Randi, and I was lucky enough to have worked voluntarily for the *James Randi Educational Foundation (JREF)* for a few years, managing their social media account back in the heady days of MySpace.

Anyway, it's around this time (2014) that the 'T' has started to be added to the LGB. This strikes me as somewhat odd, because the T is for transsexual. I understand what transsexualism is, and I also understand what sexuality is. The two are very different things. This is perhaps the first foreshadowing of what is to come.

By around 2018, I have become quite active on Twitter. I stumble across a phenomenon called 'ProAna', and I cannot believe what I'm seeing. Ana is, in case you don't know, *Ana Rexia*. The 'Pro' part signifies a movement of people who are in favour of this as a lifestyle choice. Take a moment to absorb this. There is a movement on social media which promotes anorexia as a lifestyle choice, and it is being allowed to happen, in plain sight.

The people involved post things like 'thinspo', which means *thinspiration,* an innocent sounding portmanteau disguising the ugliest of exploitations. 'Thinspo' posts feature images of dangerously underweight people who the poster says they want to look like, accompanied by hashtags like #proana #edtwt #bonespo, I've even seen #deathspo, and so it goes on. (#edtwt stands for Eating Disorder Tweets).

The posters egg each other on with things like calorie-restricted diet plans of 500 calories per day, or less, sometimes even including a starvation day once a week. They also do things like setting targets of *GW, RGW* and *UGW*. If I've translated this correctly, *GW* is Goal Weight, *RGW* is Realistic Goal Weight (this will be lower than the GW), and *UGW* is either Unrealistic or Ultimate Goal Weight.

Needless to say, UGW's come in at low double-digits in pounds and would be exceedingly unhealthy in the short term, and probably fatal if maintained for any length of time. Of course, many of these accounts are in it for the clicks, monetising the distress of the unwell. As you can probably imagine, this made my blood boil like nothing I've ever experienced before. I began to formulate a plan to make an account which exposes people conducting this evil, and to try and raise awareness for the victims of it. My dream would be if I could steer them towards getting the kind of help that might save their long-term health, because surviving anorexia doesn't mean you go physically back to normal – the effects of putting your body through that kind of stress last for the rest of your life.

I didn't know quite what approach was going to be most effective, as the 'community' (such as it is) will doubtless block any account I make that starts making waves and spreading the truth about the harm that's being done here, but these vulnerable people are being exploited, and I want try to make it stop.

And then, several things happened in quick succession. I witness people mass-attacking Graham Linehan for saying things that were clearly true. Things like, "Men cannot become women," for example. I notice my beloved community of sceptics *en masse* suddenly start professing incomprehensible things like 'Trans Women Are Women'. I saw J. K. Rowling give her support to Maya Forstater when Maya lost her job contract for saying, oh, exactly the same as Graham did.

And I saw the pictures in the Thinspo posts beginning to show mastectomy scars.

At the heart of this matter, I know that there is an overlap between anorexia and gender confusion. A few people look at their bodies and see that which is not there. Many more people look at their bodies and are violently disgusted by what they perceive. But all of us are sailing in the same boat.

One group might fixate on weight, another group may fixate on secondary sex characteristics. Both groups want to make their bodies change to reflect how they feel about themselves. The anorexics are recognised as unwell, and treatment is made available to try and help the person form a healthy relationship with their body, to come to accept it as it truly is. If the treatment is not a success, we cannot make changes to their bodies so that they permanently reflect their existing self-image, because that would mean giving a stomach staple to a person in desperate need of increased nutrition. The Hippocratic Oath states quite clearly 'do no harm'.

People with sexed-body dysphoria have a set of similar therapies available to them as well. The key difference is that there is a process by which the body can be altered, using hormones and surgeries, if all other treatment options become exhausted. This is not an easy life to pursue, but for some people the positives outweigh the difficulties, and the overall outcome is beneficial to the patient. In this situation, 'do no harm' is a summative equation, weighed out on a balance to show us the path which provides the greatest ease of pain and suffering.

The situation we find ourselves in now is one where this sensible, well-considered and balanced approach is being thrown out of the window in favour of not causing offence. Do you think I was not offended when my best friend told me I was slowly killing myself? Of course I was, deeply so. There is surely no precedent in medical history where we do not pursue the best medical outcome for the patient because it might make them upset. And yet, here we are.

Well, I for one do not want people to take body-altering hormones, or having double mastectomies, vaginoplasties and hysterectomies unless and until they have exhausted all other forms of therapy. It is my absolute belief that to do so is ethically unsound. There are people to who those procedures can be beneficial on balance, and we owe it to everyone who is affected by the deep distress that gender dysphoria causes to be absolutely certain that this is the only remaining pathway for them before they make unalterable changes to their bodies. To do otherwise is to potentially cause harm, and therefore to go against the Hippocratic Oath.

As for the so-called sceptics, well, with a few notable exceptions, they have become exemplars of what they are supposed to rally against. These people often say, "Oh, you're putting feelings over facts," when debating with those who claim, for example, to have felt the spirit of the lord move through them, or who don't accept the results of a study because it goes against their preconceived ideas.

Well, I ask those same sceptics, "Why are you so happy to put feelings over facts on this one issue? What is it about gender dysphoria that is so massively different to the dysphoria felt by an anorexic?"

"Do you believe that people have an internal Gender Identity, which is fixed, innate and immutable?" Because holy hell, that's never even been vaguely hinted at by any scientific study, ever. Not even close. Hold yourselves to the same standards you demand of others, you damned hypocrites. Don't you think that's what Randi would do, if he was still with us?

The brief for writing this piece was to tell the story of how I came to being a *gender atheist,* which is my preferred term (you can call me gender critical if you want, I won't be offended!). If I was to pinpoint one pivotal moment, it would be the J. K. Rowling tweet I mentioned above. Doubtless there will be many other people who cite this as their tipping point too. But as with all these things, there's not really one single event where I went from believer to apostate, and I hope I've been able to draw a picture for you of not only how I came to where I am today, but also why it matters so very much to me.

By way of a conclusion, I have a couple more things to say. I have not abandoned my fight against the Proana movement online. The people profiteering off the misery of others must be driven away and made both to pay for what they've done, and to demonstrate that they've learned the lesson that harming others for money is not acceptable in any society. In my view, the fight against Proana and the fight against gender ideology are intrinsically linked. The gender ideology fight is currently affecting a great many more people, has garnered enormous support and a very high profile, and my abiding hope is that the downfall of one will bring the downfall of the other. To all the people who are victims of all this, be it Proana and 'thinspo' or the gender identity confusion, please know that the people who love you are there for you, even if they find it hard to say so. Ask for help, and it WILL be there. I promise.

And so, finally, I'd like to ask a question of you, oh beloved reader. Who do you think I am? What mental picture have you formed of me as you've read through this piece? I ask this for a specific reason – because, once again I feel very much alone, almost like five-year-old me did in the school playground.

The brave people who stand every day against the harms of gender ideology are mostly women, the formidable and fearsome feminists. Standing alongside them now is a growing army of gay men, proudly returning to the fray to fight the battles they once thought were won. I give my huge respect to every one of you.

But I am not like you.

Because I am a middle-aged, straight white man. And I feel very lonely here right now. So, I end with an appeal. To all the other straight men, whatever age or race, who have remained silent on this issue. Now is the time! Come on you cowards, look at what's happening and stand up for the truth. Fight for your children, your sisters, your wives, the LGB, and most of all, fight for the young people who are caught up in this ideology right now, because a great many of them are being harmed in front of your very eyes.

Can you live with yourself if you stand by and do nothing?

• • • •

Anon

100

A safer world

My daughter going into her school and saying that she wanted to be known as a boy and the school not telling me - I was told by another parent with a child in her year, I am pretty sure that would peak most people. I won't go into detail because I don't want either myself or my daughter outed - parents like me are often vilified for not buying into gender identity ideology and affirming our children.

I requested the school's Transgender policy and it was appalling. Schools tend to buy in their policies from outside agencies who have been heavily lobbied or who are affiliated with certain (we all know who) organisations. This particular one advocated keeping information from parents who they suspect will not affirm, misrepresented Equality law (it even misrepresented GDPR), minimised the risks of hormone treatment, blockers and binders and repeatedly conflated sex and gender. I would recommend all parents with children at secondary school request to see their school's policy, it may be quite eye-opening.

Since then I have been on a bit of a voyage of discovery to try and help my daughter, she is a beautiful young girl, she just does not fit in any stereotypical boxes and there is nothing wrong with that. I resurrected a long redundant twitter account direct-messaging anyone I thought was onside and could help and going to demos and meetings.

One of the meetings was *A Women's Place* one, the one which Sharron Davies chaired talking about men in women's sport. How have we got to a place where apparently sentient people have convinced themselves that this is OK, safe or fair - madness. Another meeting was the launch conference of the *Detransitioners Network.* Speaking there were ex-Tavistock Clinicians and medical experts and then a panel of young detransitioners who spoke about their experiences and why they thought they felt the way they did. These wonderful, brave young women, talked about their mastectomies, hysterectomies, and the effects of testosterone. One thing one said, which really affected me, was that due to testosterone she had lost her singing voice. It was a very powerful event - heartbreaking and moving and it made me feel outraged that this was happening.

I think that once you become aware of one effect of this ideology, you see more and more. For example, I go regularly to *Standing for Women* events where women speak about their concerns and experiences - and have heard:-

- That they put male sex offenders in the female estate, a woman who had been in prison talked about how terrifying it was to be housed with fully intact man, under threat of sanction if she objected.

- How lesbians are being accused of bigotry by stating that they are same-sex attracted - and heard one young woman speak who was raped by a trans identified male and then vilified for speaking up about it.

- The loss of single-sex spaces and provisions, contrary to the Equality Act - e.g. schools converting their toilets to mixed-sex without bothering to consult either parents or students. One school I know of did this, and right next door to one of the newly installed mixed sex abominations, was a door with sign on it saying 'WC - Male staff only'. They seem devoid of any self awareness whatsoever.

- A woman being attacked by a trans identified male and when in court being compelled to address her male attacker with female pronouns. When she slipped up, she was sanctioned - not being awarded compensation by the Judge.

- The fact the males are being put into female wards in hospital - even psychiatric ones. When the inevitable happened and one poor woman was raped in hospital, the hospital staff said she could not have been as 'there were no men on the ward'- knowing full well there was. Why these people have not been charged with perverting the course of justice I just don't understand.

- The insidious and destructive influence of once respected charities and organisations, selling their souls to climb a meaningless champions list.

There's loads more as once your eyes are opened you can't stop seeing it all.

We are in a much better place than we were four years ago when this all started for us, mainly due to the talking therapy we have been undertaking, talking therapy, that some, who have little understanding of the issues at hand, blindly paint as conversion therapy. It is nothing of the sort and one day I sincerely hope that they will be ashamed. The tried and tested method of treatment before all this for children with gender dysphoria was always supportive 'watchful waiting' and talking therapy which resulted in an over 80% desistance rate - this percentage would likely be higher now given the recent 4,400% increase in youth identifying as trans. These children eventually growing out of their dysphoria and happy in their own skin, often as gay, lesbian or bisexual adults. To be honest then, it would be quite reasonable to think that the affirmation only approach advocated by lobby groups is what really is a form of conversion therapy.

I think we will all be OK but I will emerge from this a different person with my faith in many organisations shaken. The world is a different place now than it when this started for us - thanks largely to those wonderful brave people who stood up and said 'NO' often at great personal cost, and I cannot thank them enough. Keira Bell, Maya Forstater, Harry Miller, Kellie Jay Keen, Allison Bailey, Bayswater Support, Our Duty, Genspect, Standing for Women, Make More Noise, Sex Matters, TransgenderTrend, Fair Cop, Safe Schools, Fair Play for Women, Women's Place UK, Genspect and many more.

Kids like my daughter will be in a safer world because of you - *THANK YOU*

• • • •

JH

101

Getting away with it

Aged 40 I went to a social that I believed was for lesbians.

    I was not really 'out' and had struggled to accept my sexuality for a very long time and was hoping for a space to finally be able to try to take steps to accept myself - a few drinks with women like me.
    Instead, I got stuck with an obviously male TW (all the lesbians vanished and left me with ***, for some reason). I had no idea what was going on and how he was getting away with it. I had heard of trans people but I never thought they would be so bold as to actually claim to be lesbians. I didn't know how to get away from *** without everyone thinking I was being rude so I got stuck with ***.
    It had taken me years to build up the confidence to go at all and it all evaporated that night.

    I went home confused and upset, so I went on the internet to try to work out what was going on and if I was going mad. Sadly, I found Riley J. Dennis on YouTube along with endless other articles/videos, all telling me that I should accept male people as lesbians, increasing my distress.
    This was all in early summer 2018 at the same time Kathleen Stock gave *A Woman's Place* talk in Brighton. I couldn't believe the abuse she was getting for saying the entirely sensible things she was, especially regarding lesbians.

    I am still confused and shocked that no one in authority in mainstream so called LGBT groups will say a word to protect lesbians from this unpleasant homophobia.

• • • •

Liz

102

Asking questions

In late 2021 I listened to the BBC Nolan Investigates 'Stonewall' podcast and wanted to immediately, and loudly, ask questions in the fashion of Stephen Nolan. "What's genderfuck mean?" Stephen asked Owen Hurcum, the first openly non-binary person to be mayor of any city worldwide, based in Bangor, Wales.

The term non-binary itself is spoken about so frequently and strongly in activist circles, even in government debates. Yet there is no clear definition. Owen says, "It can mean different things to different people," and others simply say, "There's actually no rules to being non-binary." I saw a definition stating: "Non-binary strikes me as based and grounded in a very conservative view of what gender is. To identify as non-binary you're saying you don't feel male or female, but in order to not feel male or female you must have a pretty rigid idea of what male and female are and invariably those are tied to sex-stereotypes."

When I posed this to a group of real-life friends in an online space where we had regular discussions, there was anger and I was very soon after called a transphobe as the conversation was quickly shut down. A few weeks later after some further discussion on the topic I was removed from the group and they no longer speak to me. I was called hateful by some individuals that I previously respected, yet they did not have answers to what was going on.

I believed as I always had that there are only two sexes. When did that change and why was I not informed of this? But to ask questions is bad. I was soon called, 'Just asking questions guy' and 'Centrist dad'. For the crime of asking questions.

By this point in early 2022 I had looked at the numbers of children being referred to the Tavistock, another area we're not allowed to ask questions about. So I read Kathleen Stock's 'Material Girls', Helen Joyce's 'Trans: When Ideology Meets Reality' followed by Abigail Shrier's 'Irreversible Damage: The Transgender

Craze Seducing Our Daughters'. Later I started to write down what was happening in the world as reported in the news, as well as the discussions happening on Twitter.

As a born-sceptic, I have always asked questions and been doubting, questioning, incredulous. I strongly believe it is important to question belief systems. It's how I came to my atheism in my teens and the Skeptics Movement in the 2010s.

What I see today is a lot of people repeating mantras and following doctrines that they do not understand. That was never me - and never will be. We must be allowed to question what we're told to believe. Turns out when friends remove me from the group for asking these questions I will do a lot more reading. My origin to this movement comes from a support of women, a fear for what we're doing to children, and a support for LGB friends and family. As a bisexual man, I have spent time with gay friends and in gay spaces, but what is taking place is different from that and it is erasing sex and sexual orientation.

I do not support this.

Previously I had heard of 'TERFs' and was told they were bad and evil. But they are the ones who care about facts, honesty and truth over ideological thinking and bad science.

That is the side that I will stay on.

• • • •

Phil

103

A new Victorian attitude

In 2019, a small group of women from regional and rural Victoria formed *Women's Action Group*. Their motivation was the ongoing erosion of women's rights in Victoria and in all of Australia. All of these women would be considered left wing, in fact, some of them were known to each other through their unpaid work for the Victorian Greens Party. It was becoming clear that the traditional left wing parties were not prepared to protect the rights of women and girls in the face of new assaults on their rights.

The members of *Women's Action Group* headed by Michelle Uriarau, Lisa Owen and Sonia Stoneman, have campaigned tirelessly, lobbying politicians to resist changes in regulation and legislation that will bring harm to women and girls.

The main focus of that founding year was to resist the changes proposed to the Births, Deaths and Marriages Act that would allow 'sex' self ID in Victoria. They were joined in this fight, and subsequent others, by many women's groups around Australia at the time, such as the *Victorian Women's Guild, IWD Brisbane Meanjin, Women Speak Tasmania* (currently in hiatus) and *The Wagga Feminist*. Many individuals and groups of women and their allies came together to oppose transgender ideology being forced upon their communities through culture and through law. Speaking out in support of women's right to exclude men comes at a high cost for many women.

All women involved in this work have lost friends, connections with family, volunteer roles, paid jobs and whole careers.

We will persist until women are ensured of dignity, safety, fairness and autonomy in every aspect of our lives.

· · · ·

Women's Action Group, Australia

104

Watching and learning

I don't use Twitter and had no idea what was happening, how the Trans lobby was pushing for Self ID which would conflict with women's sex based rights. I saw an article in The Times, Summer 2020 which referred to J. K. Rowling being accused of transphobia for her tweet about 'People who menstruate...' and to the essay she wrote in her defence.

I guess I'd been aware at some level of the slogans 'Transwomen are women, no debate!', and of feminists being 'cancelled' but in my mind Transwomen meant men who'd had sex reassignment surgery and I would have agreed that they are women. I couldn't understand why J. K. Rowling's tweet was regarded as transphobic so I read her essay, thank you Jo Rowling for opening my eyes to the conflict between Self ID and women's rights. I was relieved when Self ID was rejected in Parliament in September that year and paid more attention to what was happening; over the next year I became aware of the issues at the Tavistock GIDs service, a very important concern for me as a trainee Social Worker – the silencing of Sonia Appleby, the concerns raised by Dr David Bell, other whistle-blowers who had left the service.

I wanted to explore this issue further – what was happening? What about other points of view? I sought out views of transwomen and came across Miranda Yardley's website. I was surprised that she doesn't refer to herself as a woman. As someone with a GRC who has had full surgery, I would respect her new identity, I found her story helped put across the conflicts clearly.

I then came across Maria MacLachlan's website and fell further down the rabbit hole, saw the horrific verbal abuse that has been launched at all the women speaking out and Maria's assault by a very masculine looking 'transwoman'.

I learnt about Autogynephilia, found that more than 90% of 'transwomen' still keep their penises, that there are men in women's prisons in the UK even though Self ID was not approved in law, female prisoners have been assaulted and raped. Crimes committed by men are being recorded and reported as having been carried out by women. Men in women's sports; I was worried I had an implicit bias so sought out the research which confirmed that men do have a physical advantage way beyond testosterone reduction. The 4,000% rise in teenage girls referred to the NHS *GIDS* (Gender Identity Development Service), I followed and supported Keira Bell's case against the Tavistock, watched Allison Bailey's tribunal, found the Mumsnet Feminism board.

I have spent hours reading reports, blogs, listening to Podcasts and watching YouTube trying to understand how this has happened, trying to find a coherent argument from the trans-activists as to why they should be treated as women when they have beards and penises and are clearly men. I found nothing but nonsense about clown fish and DSDs (differences of sexual development). How have so many Government departments and other organisations been so ignorant and so easily captured? Why are so many people denying the existence of biological sex? I feel we've all been groomed, a drip, drip of positive stories of 'trans-children', of lies about suicide rates and murder rates.

I was late to realise what was happening, and think most people are still unaware, so thank you to everyone who has been fighting against this ideology for years, for safeguarding children and fighting for women's rights; thank you J. K. Rowling, Maya Forstater, Allison Bailey, Maria MacLachlan, Julie Bindel, Magdalene Berns, Kelly Jay Keen, Graham Linehan, Emma Hilton, Helen Joyce, Jane Clare Jones, Sarah Phillimore, Stephanie Davies-Arai, Stella O'Malley, Sasha Ayad, Mumsnet feminists, Miranda Yardley, Debbie Hayton and everyone else.

Without you we would be lost already like Canada, California and so many other countries and states.

• • • •

Anon

105

Had enough

About eight or nine years ago, I remember going to a 'Gay Women's Network' event and it was hosted by a trans identified man.

At that point, I remember thinking that I didn't mind 'them' being there but was unhappy that they were in a position of authority. I remember feeling uncomfortable but also was still part of the #BeKind brigade.

About four years ago my (ex) partner decided she wanted to take testosterone/identify as 'trans'. She went from being a lesbian to calling herself 'queer'. I struggled with it – I wanted to be with a woman who was happy being a woman – I resented how her 'journey' and her identity was suddenly impacting my sexuality as she didn't like me referring to her as a lesbian or 'she' (she wanted 'they/them').

We split up not long after (we'd been together for years and the relationship wasn't working, but this was the final straw). Finally, when I started going on 'lesbian' dating sites after that break up, there were men 'identifying' as women. Men with beards who are clearly biological men. I was full of rage. I couldn't believe it. That, alongside Stonewall having the likes of Alex Drummond as 'lesbians' was just so offensive. That was the final straw for me and now my tolerance is zero for men coming into lesbian spaces, calling themselves lesbian and denying our sex based reality, oppression and sexual orientation.

I feel like the world has gone mad – I can't believe that people are bending over backwards for effectively a men's rights movement. It's misogynistic, homophobic and incredibly regressive. We need to stop this madness, but it's exhausting when political parties, institutions and corporates are buying into the narrative under the aegis of 'inclusion'.

Women – and lesbians specifically – are yet again at the bottom of the pile and I've had enough! It impacts all parts of my life and has had a damaging effect on my mental health and well being.

. . . .

Anon

106

The day I found my rage

My peak journey started off in pink sequin hot pants and kitten heels on the 6th of July 2019. It was London pride and I was darting around as 'Theresa Gay', a special incarnation of my Theresa May act, handing out leaflets for an LGBT+ campaign. It was there that I first saw the mantra 'Transwomen are women!' on a huge banner as the parade went by. I was puzzled by it - why would anyone claim that 'transwomen' were actual women?

I went online to find out more and before I knew it I'd slipped down the rabbit hole into Gender Woo Woo Land. It was a crazy place where everything was turned upside down, but thankfully I found the videos of Magdalen Berns and PeachYoghurt, as well as the voices of other women, to help me cut through the madness. I began to see the inherent misogyny and homophobia at the heart of the 'trans' movement and its harmful impact through policy, law and the subversion of language. These were the early stages of my peaking.

After about six months I began to realise how, had I been born a few decades later, my 15-year-old self would've probably embraced this gender madness as a way out of misery. Shy, insecure, depressed and at times suicidal, a mobile phone with Tumblr or TikTok would've quickly proved that the kids at school had been right all along: I wasn't actually a guy! It would've explained the bullying, the difficult relationship with my dad, why I never fit in… Off to *Mermaids* I would've gone, magical gender identity in hand, to be greeted by Susie Green. And we all know how 'effeminate' boys fare in her hands…

But my actual 'peak' came in February 2020, and violently so. I'd been working with a therapist for about a year and a half, trying to piece myself together as the memories of certain experiences had gotten the better of me. These experiences were all rooted in me being a certain type of male; the kind both the general and the gay world doesn't always look too kindly upon when masculinity is held in such high esteem. One evening, at the start of our session, he gave me a leaflet for a weekend workshop by another therapist. It was 'an experiential weekend for men to re-meet the boy they once were'.

"Sounds great!" I said. But then I turned it over and read: 'This workshop is open to anyone who identifies as a man.'

I scoffed, so the therapist asked me why. That's when it happened.

A rage I had never known began to pour out of me like a volcano erupting. I shouted, I screamed, I cursed, I cried. The therapist didn't know what was happening, and neither did I. I just felt so utterly violated by those words; like a metaphysical rape was taking place. Here I was, a man who'd learned the hard way how my very maleness had been at the heart of so much pain, ridicule, and rejection, and was working my ass off to find a way to accept myself as the man that I am – only for these word to suggest that anyone can just opt into it? All the regressive social stereotypes I'd been struggling against for decades could now simply be worn as a costume by a woman or girl and passed off as the same as me? No. No! Never! I won't let my reality be someone else's fraudulent identity. Hands off.

It took me six months to calm down. By then, I had found my peace and my voice.

And I decided to make YouTube videos.

• • • •

MrMenno

107

Stalin's 'whisperers'

My husband lost a two year music project with huge media coverage when a trans identified man involved decided to out my husband as a ' bigot'. Because my husband, (after years of knowing this man/father to three girls and close friend), politely refused to repeat the mantra 'TWAW' to prop up our friend's newly found 'identity'. (read; 'suddenly wore women's clothing and had his name changed').

As friends we patiently explained to this man that we had no issue with how he dressed, but we would not lie about his sex. We also tried to discuss the implications for women and girls under trans ideology and compelled language. It fell on deaf ears. It seemed to activate an enormous cold rage in this TIM (trans identified male)

This TIM went on to publicly shame my husband in a music industry magazine on *International Women's Day* as 'revenge'. Where he was featured as a 'woman' speaking about being discriminated against by my husband. My husband was not named, but everyone knew who was being referred to because of the precise details given.

My husband's long-time best friend 'unfriended' him shortly after this. Also calling him a 'bigot' and a 'transphobe'. Oddly this same male best friend had recently been on a blind date only to discover that the 'woman' he was meeting was actually an obvious man. He felt tricked and humiliated. which he was furious about at the time, and to which we offered tea and sympathy after the shock/ruse.

Yet, we were the 'bigots'.

The combination of all these events over a long period of time led to my husband having a heart attack. We see a connection between the stress and grief, and loss of income/musical recognition as factors that contributed to this.

We did though receive hundreds of private messages of support from many of his colleagues and friends involved in the music business. None of whom would make a public declaration of support though.

Previous to this our teen daughter, finding that the boys dominated her skateboarding park space, joined an 'All-girl skate' group. At the first meet-up she saw a 30-year-old man in a short skirt arrive for the first enrolment. He said he was a 'girl'. He was heavily overweight and couldn't even skate board.
None of the other young girl's felt brave enough to challenge him so our daughter left. He dominated the group and became their self elected 'organiser'.
This same man (married with a new baby we were to find out later) invited a group of these girls to an overnight stay/skateboarding event. He was the driver. Some of these girls invited were as young as 14 years of age. I could not understand why parents were not concerned .
Needless to say our daughter declined the 'sleepover' and the lift with this man. We have no idea what happened that night and if he stayed with these teen girls in a shared room or not.

Previous to this event our daughter had been purged from her large social circle for refusing to call her male 6-feet-tall friend a 'girl'. Various friends approached our daughter telling her she MUST use female pronouns for him 'or else'. This male friend, though gentle and sweet, suffered from severe anxiety and was on the spectrum. Someone who really didn't fit in and had a lovely head of long dark hair which he was bullied for by other boys.
His mother encouraged and endorsed his new 'trans identity, to the point that we felt this 'identity' was driven by her own narcissism and not her son's confusion. She also spearheaded the campaign for mixed-sex bathrooms (gender neutral) at the College our daughter was due to attend. Our daughter was no longer invited to any of her friend's birthday parties or outings. Any pleas made by her to meet and talk were met with silence. She suffered huge anxiety and depression shortly after this.
Her confidence was shattered, but she did stand her ground. We are very proud of her for doing this at such a tender age when friends mean everything. It has been a good life lesson. And she may well be vindicated in time .

Entire families connected to this purging then blanked us

as a family in our local village. Literally turning their backs on us if we crossed paths in a supermarket. Parents whose children I had fed, comforted and had over for sleepovers and holidays growing up over many years.

When I raised the issue privately within my local *People Before Profit* group I was told I was to leave and that I was 'Alt-right'. The woman who ran this branch ended my close friendship with her by email, telling me my views were not acceptable.

Shortly afterwards I was heckled as I left the local Tesco one dark night alone… by a stranger who shouted, "Terf Bitch" and drove away.

Other friends and extended family members drifted away or told me they were, 'horrified' by my stance. There were some upsetting scenes at one Christmas Dinner. The rift has never healed.

That stance that was so appalling to others was simply the centring of the rights of girls to safety dignity and privacy from men in their sports, spaces and by compelled language.

Stalin's 'whisperers' who were told to snitch on family and neighbours for ' wrongthink', wouldn't get a look in when judged against the cruelty and incoherence of our own friends and neighbours and the 'Left' leaning political parties we once adhered to.

* * * *

Anon

108

Then the eyes of the blind shall be opened

I was in a pub in 2017 and I heard a lovely young barman grouched at by a woman for calling her 'she'.

"DON'T ASSUME MY GENDER," she scolded. I said to my husband, "But she IS a she". He said, "You sound like a terf".
"What's a terf?" I asked.

Over the next few months I was seeing more stuff on Twitter and thinking, "Well, this can't be happening. Who would look at this man and think he's a woman?"

Later in the year I read about Helen Steele at the *Anarchist Book Fair* defending a woman from nasty bullies for feminist leaflets. And Maria MacLachlan got hit by that thug 'Wolf'.

The scales rapidly fell after that

• • • •

Hackney Terven

109

I read everything I could find

I could have been on board with trans rights. I would have been on board if it was about opposing unfair and illegal discrimination. In fact that's what I assumed was happening, back when I first started hearing the phrase 'trans rights' in the media.

Then Jenni Murray got into trouble for saying something perfectly obvious. Then I heard Ed Miliband do a podcast about trans rights. It was unashamedly one-sided. There was a passing mention of a conflict with feminists and I wondered what that was about. I decided it was worth finding out. I read from every point of view I could find: transactivists, transsexuals, those describing themselves as transgender, detransitioners, feminists who were on board with current transactivism, feminists who opposed it, those who live with differences of sex development, healthcare professionals who support child transition and those who oppose it, mental health professionals from either side of the debate, academics, philosophers, journalists, academic papers, spouses and children of transitioners... *everything I could find*.

Out of that reading a clear picture emerged. Modern trans-activism is not about opposing discrimination for those who have distress over their sexed bodies. It is about imposing a novel claim about a hypothetical 'gender identity' on all of us: that what makes us male or female (or both, or neither, or something else) is not the fact of having a male or female body, but is determined by our gender identity. If you believe in gender identity, fair play to you - you are free to believe what you like. But I don't, and I have the freedom to disbelieve.

What I observed were transactivists who had neither reasonable nor coherent arguments for their position, and who resorted to evidence-free assertions, bullying, and threats towards anyone who didn't fall into line with their beliefs or who refused to parrot their mantras. I found solid arguments opposing their position that were well-constructed, evidenced and reasonable.

The (mainly) women who made these arguments were subject to appalling abuse.

I looked around at the real-world consequences of the transactivist political movement. I saw that laws and policies had been changed with little to no knowledge of these changes among the general public. I discovered that had been a deliberate strategy. I saw men placed in female prisons and men competing in female sports. I saw political positions reserved for women going to men. I saw female-only spaces and services being lost in the name of so-called inclusivity, despite the move to mixed-sex facilities driving away women who were in need of the single-sex provision. I saw my daughters had lost their female-only toilets at school and were now trying to avoid using the school toilets, and if they went on overnight trips they'd be in 'same gender' accommodation, which could be mixed-sex.

I realised that the end point of transactivism, in re-defining us in terms of gender identity and doing away with sex as a relevant variable, means erasing the category that protects women in law. Does an organisation pay females less? How can you tell when all you record is self-defined gender? Are the employment practices unfavourable to women? How can you tell when all you record is self-defined gender? Need a same-sex medical professional? Will you be provided with a same-sex or a same 'gender' practitioner?

Sex is one of nine protected characteristics in UK law. To do away with it by replacing it with gender identity is to strip us of the ability to observe, record, and oppose discrimination against women and girls. Transactivism, by accident or design, is a movement of misogyny.

• • • •

Anon

110

O no Canada!

I owe the honing of my gender critical faculties to *The Feminist Current*, the only Canadian online publication that consistently recognizes women as a sex class and carried the torch for Second Wave women like me.

Its writers showed me the path that gender ideology took through almost all of Canada's institutions and public discourse, pointing out its corrupting influence on our legislature, public education, prison systems and healthcare. Thanks to *The Current* I could see the ideology's handiwork at the federal level, when in 2018 the original *Status of Women Canada* was renamed '*The Department of Women and Gender Equity*', signalling to all that our government could no longer define what a woman is!

> Canadian Women's Sex-Based Rights - caWsbar
> @cawsbar · Follow
>
> According to **@WAGE_FEGC** (formerly Status of Women), the Government of Canada now claims not to know what a woman is.
>
> "WAGE does not use a specific definition of 'woman'."
>
> #cdnpoli #BillC16

Critics of gender ideology are considered a kind of deadly Plutonium, according to our legacy media. So to my outrage the publisher of *The Current*, Meghan Murphy herself was pilloried or ignored by the CBC. Twitter banned her, and she was vilified and harassed online and in public at every turn.

But this outrage is nothing compared to the moral injury this ideology delivered to my family's doorstep. A young female relative, who had declared herself a lesbian in her early teens, then proceeded to bind her breasts for years. As soon as she turned eighteen, she had a double mastectomy.

The news of her surgery hit me hard, like a bruising blow to the heart.

It took me a year to figure out her motives, some of which could well have been my own had I been a teen today and social media's creature. In her case a lesbian is just another porn genre, so she was still subject to the male gaze. In both our cases there had been sexual abuse. A double mastectomy presents the ultimate cure, an exit from a humiliating womanhood, from being forever a thing and the target of sexual predators.

She like so many other women of her generation bear the scars from a battle I thought had already been won on women's behalf. But no, we've obviously lost ground. So I've had to re-commit to today's women's movement and take up the fight for our rights again!

. . . .

Anon

111

I thought Mermaids was a swimming club!

How does a quiet woman, nearing 60, get into all this? Basically, I blame Radio 4.

I was an addict until I realised how much they weren't telling us. But this day in November 2017, I was working with *The Moral Maze* on in the background.

I can't actually recall listening closely to what was being said but stopped to listen intently when a mild-mannered woman seemed to be urging caution regarding the transitioning of children.

It wasn't what she said, it was hearing the shouts of 'TERF' from the audience that was shocking. I'd never heard heckling from the audience on that programme before and it was pretty unpleasant. As far as I'd heard she had said nothing wrong. Clare Fox, a hero of mine, was on too and her last words were, "The world has gone mad!" The two men seemed to be saying it was harmful not to do what children wanted.

After the programme the speaker was expelled from her political party - *The Women's Equality Party* - for 'transphobia'. What on earth was going on? I really knew nothing. I thought Mermaids was a swimming club! I already was on Twitter so I got myself educated pretty quickly. Boggling at the abuse towards women for stating their belief in biology. Everything they said seemed to get the same reaction: verbal abuse, belittling and general character assassination.

I'd never knowingly mixed with Radical Feminists before. In fact they scared me in case I said something wrong. Same with LGBTI - another eggshell territory as far as I was concerned. Suddenly I was watching both camps. It really didn't take long to realise that I agreed with the feminists and that they were brave, funny and highly articulate. I was in awe of the way they weren't intimidated by their aggressors. Later I realised that one gets used to it and the more attempts at silencing, the more determined one becomes.

Anyway, I became a reluctant participator telling myself that as soon as we'd seen off Self-ID I could go back to a peaceful, quiet life. Life isn't really like that. The more I learnt, the more alarmed I became. It wasn't just Self-ID, it was the harming of children and young people and the almost total ideological capture of the whole establishment that was so terrifying.

Maria, in court, being instructed to address the man who assaulted her using female pronouns was an important moment. Being told that I was now to be called 'cis' was another one. Reading one woman's story about having to leave a refuge when they made it clear inclusion would mean they'd welcome men from now on. Another moment of fury was hearing of a nurse whose manager told her to 'just get on with it' when a trans identified male demanded she perform a smear. What?!! I'd been a nurse for a long time and the idea that female patients were being labelled as transphobic for objecting to males sharing their ward was another injustice I vowed to fight.

Twitter was removing hundreds of women from the platform for 'misgendering' or insisting sex cannot be changed. Jonathan Yaniv, clearly a man who then called himself 'Jessica' would entrap many and get them banned. He asked, "Was he a woman?", and being an honest sort of woman, I said, "No". He said. "You'll get banned for that," and within the hour I was. Very annoying as I had a great business account and had just got my business cards printed. Still, small inconvenience really.

The Government extended the GRA consultation deadline yet still it wasn't being covered by the main media. Woman's Hour avoided any mention. Without these brave women sounding the alarm, we would certainly have had self-ID brought in. Almost all the Labour Party described the trans groups as vulnerable and marginalised - it would take very little detective work to show this wasn't true.

Miranda Yardley, a trans identified male, was taken to court by a high profile member of Mermaids, for transphobia! You honestly could not make this up. His crime was to be on the side of women. Luckily the case was thrown out quickly but it caused him a huge amount of stress - the punishment is the process.

Posie Parker was visited and interviewed under caution for saying that Susie Green of Mermaids had taken her 16-year-old son to Thailand for castration. True, but not allowed to be said. Harry Miller was told to 'check his thinking' by the police after retweeting a rhyme that upset the trans lobby. It was obvious something indeed was rotten in the State of Denmark.

Gradually groups were set up to address specific areas of concern. *Transgender Trend, Safe Schools Alliance, Standing for Women, Keep Prisons Single Sex.*
Apart from my family, being a member of *Fair Cop* has been my proudest achievement. It seems a long time ago that Rob Jessel tweeted about protesting against the ideological capture of the police and who else would be interested?
To get the police to serve without fear and favour is the aim. Harry Miller and Sarah Phillimore perfectly compliment each other and have made the group a real force to be reckoned with. Some way to go but the victories are significant.

Sometimes it seems that we will never win the fight against this pernicious ideology that says that children can be born in the wrong body, that women's safety, dignity and rights do not matter. That anyone who says otherwise should be deprived of their livelihoods and their character destroyed.

But British resisters have already achieved a huge amount and their courage and determination counts for a great deal more than money. We lead the world in the fight back.

We can do this.

And we will.

. . . .

Anon

112

It is by women and by land, that the people are given life

(He wāhine, he whenua ka ora te tangata)

"In te ao Māori there is a synergy between women and land, and that without one or the other or both, man (humanity) will not survive. The representation of wāhine, therefore (sic), is a wider discussion about land and the continuation of whakapapa."

2018 M. Eria, 'Te ao Māori :
The synergy between women and the land'

Of all the profound questions posed to humankind throughout time, no one could have guessed that the question, "What is a woman?" would be one of them. Especially as the question itself is not profound at all. Yet the trending narrative that 'anyone can be a woman' is now considered a truth to the point that major changes have recently been passed into New Zealand law that allows men to legally falsify the nominated sex on their birth certificate, hiding evidence of their actual sex. The new law allows them to be legally recognised as a woman based on nothing more than a personal declaration.

Unlike previous stringent conditions, the requirements to provide medical evidence, and undergo years of therapy and radical surgery have been removed. In other words, no man needs to change a thing about his appearance to legally be considered a 'woman'.

The Big Lie, typically credited to Goebbels, comes to mind. To say it is surreal to witness everyone in New Zealand's parliament acquiesce to the bizarre and perilous doctrine that is gender identity is an understatement, although NZ is not the only Government to have done so. Even more puzzling is the seemingly docile complicity by elitist Māori to go along with the popular, yet deceitful, allegation that tamariki and mokopuna (children and grandchildren) can be born in the wrong bodies.

What a time to be alive!

On page three of *Te Ara*, the Encyclopedia of New Zealand, in 'Sexual Diversity in Contemporary Māori Society', Clive Aspin makes the claim:

'...transgender people hold a revered position within Māori society. Transgender people play an important role within both the takatāpui community and wider Māori community as holders and transmitters of ancestral knowledge.'

Who are these so-called 'transgenders' that Aspin refers to? Which hapū (sub-tribe)? Which whakapapa (descendancy) are they from and what exactly does he mean by 'transgender'? On the other hand we have the seemingly infrequently read, but gratuitously marketed, PhD thesis by Dr Elizabeth Kerekere, in which she makes a complete 180 degree turn to the above statement by Clive Aspin on page 82 in her thesis, to state that:

'There is not yet evidence that Māori had diverse gender identities or that tākatāpui played specific roles in pre-colonial times.'

Clearly there is a disconnect between what we are being told by both Aspin and Kerekere, who are at odds with each other, and what is reality in relation to Te Ao (Māori world view) and Tikanga Māori (customs, values and practices). Those of us raised within our culture know that we have always been defined by hapū established by whakapapa. Our culture has always been passed down to us by our kaumatua (elders) NOT academics or politicians. Broad sweeping baseless claims about 'Māori' can become quickly unravelled when specifics of hapū and whakapapa are either vague or non-existent.

Gender-identity ideology originated out of American academia and threatens that everyone must invest in its most outlandish, impractical and unrealistic beliefs - even those who work within government departments. The Regulatory Impact Statement for the Sex-Self ID Bill, which was recently passed into law, claimed that (p12, 32.):

'Only recognising binary genders may have had a negative impact specific to Māori. Research suggests that there was gender diversity within Te Ao Māori and that has diminished with colonisation. This has negatively affected the acceptance and participation of gender diverse Māori in their own communities.'

This is a direct appropriation of our culture. So, why did Māori Members of Parliament who have the power to take the Government to task over such ridiculous claims, remain silent on the matter?

I can only speculate.

The truth is that there is no haka, no waiata, no mōteatea, no whakataukī and no whakairo that proves that diverse gender identities ever existed in Te Ao and in pre-colonial times for Māori. Humans can never change sex. Regardless of culture, lying to any child about biological reality is incredibly cruel. How a child feels on any given day should never be responded to with off-label cancer drugs to stop their natural pubertal development or radical surgical amputation of their healthy breast or penile tissue. The very idea is horrific to the point of insanity, yet it has been written into New Zealand law. The answer to the question 'what is a woman' is of course, **wāhine: adult human female**.
Only wāhine can bring forth life which is why only wāhine can karanga (make the call of welcome). In 'The Man Called to Karanga' which aired on Māori Television in 2018, Pita Tamiana's mother told him, men do not karanga because it attracts death. Unsurprisingly, Pita discounts his mother's advice and wisdom, perhaps because he is academically trained? I am not sure, but the emerging picture of our culture being contaminated by certain academics and politics instead of being governed and guided by hapū and kaumatua, as is our custom, is an unsettling one.

Sisters Phillippa, Di and Rex Landy (Ngāti Kahu) and I are founding members of Mana Wāhine Kōrero. We are the only indigenous group created by indigenous women to advocate for the safeguarding of our wāhine, tamariki, mokopuna and our cultural integrity primarily against gender-identity propaganda.

We refuse to capitulate to this ideology which inserts itself uninvited into our culture, erases our mana (sovereignty) as wāhine and hijacks our ability to safeguard in law that which we hold dear above all else; our tamariki and mokopuna.

How can tangata whenua (the people) survive when this ideology seeks to permanently end the continuation of our whakapapa through the castration of our children and grandchildren?

When I am asked about this topic "Why are you so angry?",

I respond, *"Why are you not!"*

. . . .

Michelle Uriarau - Ngāti Hinepare, Ngāti Mahu, Ngāti Kahungunu

113

What the Dickens is going on?

It was the best of times, *it was the worst of times, it was the age of wisdom, it was the age of foolishness, it was the epoch of belief, it was the epoch of incredulity, it was the season of light, it was the season of darkness, it was the spring of hope, it was the winter of despair.*

Charles Dickens describes best my journey from blissful ignorance to fully-fledged TERF.

Looking back, I'm amazed how long it took me to see what was happening. But I was working full-time, and I am a mother, so I just wasn't paying attention. Mine was a bizarre baptism of fire because I have no interest in following sport - but it was sport that dragged me into the 'Trans Debate' in February 2019. Specifically, an article by *The Independent*'s chief sportswriter, Jonathan Liew.

I can't even remember how I came across it but I remember the impact. "They're coming! Over the horizon, they're coming! They're coming for your medals and your trophies and your endorsement contracts. They're coming, with their giant bulging muscles and enormous flapping penises, to ruin everything pure and good", he wrote.

I would have laughed my tits off - if he hadn't then launched into the most condescending and repulsive attack on women who merely wanted safety and fairness in the sports they loved; culminating in the words: "Because trans women are women. And sport, I'm afraid, is only sport."

I couldn't believe what I was reading...The CHIEF BLOODY SPORTSWRITER of a national newspaper was actually saying in print that *sport is only sport*. Of course, what he meant was women's sport was only women's sport... not worthy of protecting or bothering about.

My epoch of incredulity

I reactivated my dormant Twitter account, found an avatar, thought up a Twitter handle and "educated myself" about the trans issue - and, boy, what an education it was. Men in women's prisons, their toilets and their changing rooms. In their rape crisis centres and on their hospital wards.

I read about a man, Munroe Bergdorf, who tweeted in 2018 that to 'centre reproductive systems' at London's Women's March was 'reductive and exclusionary. And I found out that Philip Bunce, who part-time cross-dressed at work, was named on the Financial Times & HERoes Champions of Women in Business list, a yearly ranking of 100 company leaders who support women in business.

WTAF? You're having a fucking laugh.

I never looked back.

My winter of despair

Much about gender ideology is laughable... the ridiculous men in lipstick with their badly-fitting wigs, stubble, fishnet tights and skanky bedrooms; their heads tilted as they 'skirts-go-spinny' among the discarded clothes and used tissues. Do they even play that shit back before they press send?

But for every farce, there is a tragedy. The transing of children. The horrific medicalisation, sterilisation and mutilation of young bodies. The 5,000% rise in girls identifying as boys with nobody in charge asking why. As I write, there are 41,000 women and girls crowdfunding for 'top surgery' on *GoFundMe* alone.

Despite the assurances from organisations such as Mermaids that puberty blockers are reversible, they are not - and they are far from safe. I read about 'Leo', who was treated by the Karolinska University Hospital in Sweden and who now hasn't grown, who has osteopenia, spinal fractures and is in constant pain. Leo was one of 13 children at that clinic who have suffered irreversible damage. How could I walk away from this?

The season of light

Thankfully, as time has gone on, light has been shone on the dark side of gender ideology. I've read everything by JK Rowling... truly, *the witch they couldn't burn.* The tribunals of Maya, Allison, Raquel and others have helped expose how far the tentacles of Stonewall have embedded themselves in organisations and the corporate world. Big shout-out too for Stephen Nolan and his Stonewall podcast which brought us Owen Hurcum, the funniest mayor since H'angus the Monkey.

The spring of hope

I've read books and essays and blogs and listened to as many podcasts as I can. And I've networked and protested at meetings and marches. I've dressed up as a dinosaur and designed posters and banners. I've emailed the House of Lords and my MP. I've live-tweeted tribunal cases for Tribunal Tweets on Twitter.

And we're winning.

I won't rest until we have got our words, spaces, sports and children back but I think we're past the worst of times. I see light at the end of the tunnel. We have wisdom, logic, science, laughs and Tunnocks teacakes to keep us going.

Thanks and love to all of the Terven wherever you live - in different circumstances, this would be purely the best of times. And, of course, Viva Terf Island!

• • • •

TerfyMcTerfyFace

114

Fighting monsters in the dark

Unlike most people, I did not have a specific moment where I 'peaked' and suddenly realised that something awful was going on. This is at least in part because I used to be heavily invested in queer theory. My PhD cited Judith Butler and 'queered' binaries. I taught *Gender Trouble* to undergraduates. I campaigned successfully to change the LGB group I led to 'LGBT'. I put a successful motion to the Student's Union to get rid of the Women's Officer and instate two 'Gender Officers'. I believed sex to be a spectrum and used people with disorders of sexual development as human shields in defence of that belief. I regarded myself as pansexual and polyamorous. I was heavily involved in BDSM, and in all sorts of other dysfunctional, dysregulated behaviour around alcohol, drugs, pornography and promiscuity. I was so up to my neck in queer theory that at one point I even dyed my hair blue.

I believed what I was doing to be binary-breaking, full of meaning, exploratory of 'limit experiences', alive with a proliferation of liminal spaces, and embodying of the theory that I was studying. This was not the truth. It was a rationalisation. In fact, I was using a variety of terrible coping mechanisms to try and avoid having to face the sexual abuse I suffered throughout my childhood. Just as recovering from what happened to me has been a long process, rooting out queer theory brain worms is not something I did in one fell swoop. Rather, a series of changes I made in my personal life led to realisations about my unhelpful political beliefs.

Here I set out a few of them.

Limit Experiences

Limit experiences are extreme experiences such as grief, certain sexual experiences, and particularly sadomasochistic ones, where the idea of the self as a coherent whole dissolves. I used to seek this kind of sexual experience constantly. It led me to some dangerous situations, but I didn't care. I would not accept anybody policing my desires.

When I was 24, I met my wife. She made it clear early on that she expected me to be faithful to her. I didn't do monogamy. But she insisted. And for reasons unbeknownst to me, instead of telling her to fuck off, I said, "Alright then," and drove her to Newcastle to see my favourite painting.
Later, nestled in that spot between the curve of her breast and the strength of her arm, I told her a little of what happened to me and cried. I don't think I've ever seen her so angry, before or since. She said, "How dare he? I hope his cock rots off. You're so strong and so beautiful... Look at you. How fucking dare he?" and she let me feel the strength of her arms around me.
Then she kissed the tears from my face and everything was better. And without saying a word, she let me know that I was still beautiful to her. That she still loved me. That she didn't think I was dirty or wrong or broken. Then she kissed me some more, put her healing hands on all the places I had been hurt, and I experienced something completely new to me; real, deep, raw, physical desire, all mixed up with love and intimacy and vulnerability and a joy that burst out of me like a song of praise.

All the dysregulated, dissociated, dysfunctional sex I had been having paled into insignificance next to that. It was an embodied, physical experience that presented me with clear evidence of what I think I always suspected – that the BDSM, kink, poly, porn, the whole lot was all a damaging waste of time for me. That I had just been an abused girl seeking ways to recreate the conditions of her abuse. I didn't want to hurt any more, I wanted the harbour of her hands. It was not an intellectual departure from that particular bit of queer theory. Not at all.

Binary Thought

According to Queer Theory, Western thought is structured by binaries. Light and dark, good and evil, male and female. 'Queering', or disrupting these binaries is one of the goals of queer theory. As a survivor of childhood sexual abuse, whose whole personality was pretty much structured around these boundary difficulties, I relished taking every opportunity to 'queer' other people's bourgeois binary distinctions.

There isn't a clear distinction between friends and lovers; Don't you love your friends? And all types of love can be expressed through physical contact. There isn't a distinction between sexual touch and other types of touch. One kind of touch might be sexual for you and not the other person. A hug can be both. Why is genital contact always sexual? What about breastfeeding? Biological sex doesn't matter. What does it matter what somebody has in their pants if you're blindfolded and they're using their hands?

It is obvious to me now what I was doing. I was not arguing that the existence of dawn and dusk meant that day and night were indistinguishable, I was creating a series of excuses for my dysregulated behaviour as a direct result of sexual abuse.

Most children understand the difference between children and adults, the difference between acceptable physical contact between friends, family members, and professionals. Most have a natural 'ick' towards everything related to sex, from the time they first understand what it is until puberty kicks in. In order to abuse a child, a molester usually has to overcome boundaries that children already have in place. I was shown violent pornography from the age of seven. There were no consistent boundaries around appropriate touching in the house I grew up in. I didn't do body or relationship boundaries. I had no ick to overcome.

As an adult, I couldn't own my vulnerability because I couldn't live in a world where I could be raped again. Most of all, I couldn't live in a world where people who should have protected me just turned their eyes away. So I never said 'no' to sex. I let myself be hurt over and over. I justified it by all my boundary-blurring queer theory talk.

But I knew I wanted children. I knew it in my heart, my guts, my womb, in every single cell of my body. At a visceral level, I knew I could not do a good job of raising children, boys or girls, unless I sorted out my boundary issues. Queer theory boundary-breaking, liminality was fine for me, I reckoned, but I did not want it for my children. So I started to read.

I read about how to raise children. I read about sleep schedules and how boundaries made children feel safe and loved. I wept for the child I was, who missed out on all the boundaries that are so helpful for children to learn. My body and yours, parent and child, appropriate and inappropriate touching. I studied how to show children you love them whilst also holding up boundaries for them like it was a foreign language. I will be a stranger in this foreign land until I die. No matter how familiar I am with the customs and the language, this will never really be my home. And love and boundaries will never be my mother tongue.

But I worked so hard at my fluency. Harder than I ever have at anything in my life. I practiced, and I thought it all through, over and over, every day. I read and practiced, read and practiced. I still do. And somehow, by some miracle, my children speak the language of love and boundaries with the ease and fluency that I could never master. It is my second language, but they learned it at my knee. It is their mother tongue.

As the years passed and my children grew, it became more and more obvious that I was right to have rejected queer theory. It became more and more obvious that my former beliefs and practices were incompatible with the protection of children from the predation of adults. And slowly the realisation came - over years and perhaps over a decade - that if it had not been good enough for my children, then it had not been good enough for me. It was not an intellectual realisation. Not at all.

Saying No

When I was brutally beaten and raped as a young teenager, I learned that my 'no' was so meaningless that I might as well give up saying it. If I never said no, nobody could rape me again. If I never had needs, or asserted myself, nobody could ever let me down or be angry with me. My default was always to choke down my 'no' and change something about myself to accommodate those who would tread on me. Set myself on fire to keep others warm. Lie down in front of the door and write 'doormat' on my head, then get resentful that others were wiping their feet on me. Learning to say "no" ushered in a turbulent period in my marriage, my relationship with my family of origin, my job, and my friendship groups. But being able to say 'no' and bloody well mean it, perhaps more than anything else, has given me a sense of myself, of who I am and what I am worth.

I had learned a lot about which lines were being crossed and who was paying the price (always women in shelters, sports, and so on). I was starting to see how Queer Theory and gender ideology had become Trojan horses for dangerous men and sex offenders to get access to children. I kept my silence about my own history or mentioned it only obliquely down in the comments. And then the *Wi Spa* incident happened. A man with a history of sexual offending went into the women's changing room at a spa and waved his penis about in front of women and girls. A brave woman confronted first the man, then the staff. It was caught on video. The staff and the helpful passer-by sided with... *the man.*

I got so furious. I sat on my sofa grinding my teeth and seething well into the night. I knew that this was not a transwoman. I knew that the woman who had said 'no' to this man was in the right. I knew that he was a sex offender. And I knew that he was swinging his dick for sexual kicks. I couldn't read and I couldn't think I went to bed fuming. I don't know what happened that night but the next morning I woke up, told my wife not to talk to me, lifted my computer, and typed out a thread on Twitter. I called the man a predator. I was brave enough to say what happened to me when I was a kid. I called out those who were saying that the victim should have 'averted her eyes'. I affirmed in public what I decided before my children were born – that little people would be safe around me, that I would never avert my eyes. I wrote a big, bold 'no' on my Twitter account.

It is still my pinned tweet for that reason.

But I could never have recognised what really happened at the *Wi Spa* unless I had learned to say 'no' in a way that matters.

In defence

I had to find a way not just to live in a world where there are monsters - men - who like to hurt little children for fun. I had to find a way to live in a world where every single adult in my life half knew what was happening and not one was willing or able to help me. A world with monsters may be difficult and dark, but it can be a fairy tale so long as there is somebody willing to confront the evil. A knight with a sword. A brave princess. But there was nobody. I lived in a corridor with endless doors, and behind every door was a monster. I ran back and forth and closed each door as it creaked open, but I was so tired. And when I lay down to sleep, the doors flew open and the monsters came for me. I was a little girl again, back in those rooms where I thought I would die, wrestling monsters in the dark. I did not want to live in that world, but I didn't see how I could escape. In therapy I got a little bit brave. I opened the doors to each of those rooms in turn. I faced the monster. I faced him not as a frightened, vulnerable, powerless little girl, but as an adult. I stood strong and the monster hid his face in shame and scurried away. And then I realised something. All that time I had been closing the doors to those rooms, I had been closing somebody in with the monsters. I realised that somebody was younger me. So I wrenched her out of those rooms. I wrapped my arms round her and made her safe. Brought her back to my garden, to my heart. She's here with me now as I write this. As real to me as you are. And never was a little girl so warm and safe and well beloved as she is in my heart. What my therapist realised - but I did not - was that through the process I was recreating myself as a human being. I was becoming the adult who I needed when I was a little girl. I was making myself brave. I was building my own sword and shield and learning how to wield them. I was becoming unafraid of monsters, able to look them in the face, stare them down, force them to own their own shame. I was becoming strong and boundaried and brave. I don't live in a corridor any more, and there are no monsters, no closed doors. I am in a walled garden, in the sunshine, where my children play.

So how do I deal with living in a world where there are monsters? Where almost everybody averts their eyes and sacrifices up little children instead of rocking the boat? I have survived by becoming the kind of adult I needed in my life when I was a little girl. When I am brave enough to talk about my experiences of surviving childhood sexual abuse, survivors message me and say, "thank you" and, "I feel less alone". And I say, "I hope the bastard's cock rots off" and, "it wasn't your fault".

When I talk about how to recognise child molesters, women message me and tell me that they've got rid of their boyfriend. That their children are safe in their beds because their mother read my threads, got wise, got brave, and took action.

All of this makes it hard to set out a way to debate the other side on substantive issues. I believe that many activists campaigning to the hard won rights and protections enjoyed by women, children and LGB people are simply doing what I did – latching on to a theory which provides a rationalisation for their dysfunctional behaviour.

Changing their minds may require the kind of change of heart that I experienced. It may, in fact, not be possible. But in the end, we do not have to change their minds. Who cares what a person is thinking whilst they are holding the door open for child molesters and perverts? We don't have to persuade them of anything.

We simply have to defeat them.

• • • •

Ceri Black

Watching the TERFS

First off I'm 'Jessie' from Shonagh Dillons blog: *A Scottish Sister Speaks - Shonagh Dillon.* When I did this with Shonagh, I was under suspension and investigation from my employer, S*cottish Women's Aid,* for raising safeguarding concerns about an Advisory Panel regarding them allowing any self identifying or non-binary individual to take part in a group for 16 to 25-year-olds. I kept my name out until that was concluded but I am me on Twitter: *verdiwilson@verdimurray.*

I've been public now for a very long time. They couldn't sack me but I was told I had to shut up and put up, so I resigned. I fully expected what came my way. I did it how I did to make sure I had evidence of just how dreadful things are in the *Violence Against Women* sector. It was quite shocking to realise no one really cared except those of us who know what is at stake.

I'd worked on the domestic abuse helpline for years and I've done various work with regards to women's rights for longer than I care to admit to.

Originally (about a decade ago)I was a supporter of transwomen being included. Back when there was trust that a process was undertaken and safeguarding process followed. After attending the WPUK meeting in Edinburgh years ago I got the wake up call.

Recently, there was an advert for an advisory panel put out. At first glance it said 'women and girls' but in the small print it was transwomen, non binary, gender-fluid, etc. I made a comment on twitter that it should be made clear this is a mixed-sex panel.

I make no mention of my work on Twitter but the user name IS my real name.

I was going to raise this at work. I knew it would cause ructions as any mention of GRA reform used to cause people to scatter in the office. I've had a number of quiet conversations about how this seems odd.

I went to look up the person in charge of the advert and stumbled across an open discussion on teams that was awful. I kick myself for only taking one snapshot. it was clear that calling certain women's organisations hateful and anti-trans was very popular! Half the main office staff were involved.

I openly posed the question of why it hasn't been made clear that the advisory group is mixed-sex as there are serious safeguarding issues having abused 16 to 25-year-olds in a room with men. My manager commented they would address this with me privately.

That conversation got me suspended and investigated.

I hadn't done anything wrong so they couldn't sack me. However it was made very clear I would be getting an eye kept on me and I need to support the position they have that sex does not exist as a real thing.

I resigned.

Being told to put up and shut up is not a form of feminism I recognise. I could afford to lose my job as I have other work but this is what's going on.

I work relief for *Edinburgh Women's Aid* too and have currently been ghosted. But I'll be leaving them too.

I no longer recognise the women's aid movement in Scotland. And I'd be surprised if any working class women will be employed by *Scottish Women's Aid* under the present management.

It's awful.

My resignation letter:

To Whom It May Concern,

Following on from what has been a distressing and depressing period of employment, I hereby tender my resignation, effective immediately.

Seeing the anti-feminist conversation from five individuals was beyond shocking. Given the very open nature of that conversation and the course of action taken against me for raising safe guarding issues around the advisory panel demonstrates that Scottish Women's Aid is no longer an organisation with feminism at its core. Sisterhood has always been complicated but we should always support women's right to discuss politics whether we agree with them or not rather than silencing them, lurking on social media and using slurs.

Scottish Women's Aid's position, that it no longer believes sex is a reality, needs to be made clear to the public. Transwomen have been included in our work for many years but now deciding to include gender non-binary, etc. into work supposed to be about women renders that work meaningless with regards to sex based violence. It also means that vulnerable women are at very real risk of being in a room with a male against their will. I cannot sit in silence for another case like that of Kristi Hanna or Karen White to happen and it seems that common sense has been usurped by gender ideology.

As I can no longer fully stand behind the work of Scottish Women's Aid , something which has pained me greatly to come to terms with, I will continue my work for women's rights and equality elsewhere.

Yours faithfully,

Verdi Wilson

• • • •

*   *   *   *

End

Transpositions

Personal journeys into gender criticism

Printed in Great Britain
by Amazon